ENGLISH for COMPUTER SCIENCE

Norma D. Mullen
P. Charles Brown

Oxford University Press

Oxford University Press
Walton Street, Oxford OX2 6DP

London New York Toronto Delhi Bombay
Calcutta Madras Karachi Kuala Lumpur Singapore
Hong Kong Tokyo Nairobi Dar es Salaam
Cape Town Melbourne Auckland

and associated companies in
Beirut Berlin Ibadan Mexico City Nicosia

OXFORD is a trade mark of Oxford University Press

ISBN 0 19 437650 8

© Oxford University Press 1984

First published 1984
Third impression 1984

All rights reserved. No part of this publication may be
reproduced, stored in a retrieval system, or transmitted,
in any form or by any means, electronic, mechanical,
photocopying, recording, or otherwise, without the
prior permission of Oxford University Press.

This book is sold subject to the condition that it shall
not, by way of trade or otherwise, be lent, re-sold, hired
or otherwise circulated without the publisher's prior
consent in any form of binding or cover other than that
in which it is published and without a similar condition
including this condition being imposed on the
subsequent purchaser.

Filmset in Plantin by
Filmtype Services Limited,
Scarborough, North Yorkshire.

Printed in Hong Kong.

Acknowledgements

Special thanks are extended to Douglas J. Potvin, Director of the Centre for Continuing Education, Concordia University, Montreal, and the staff of the Continuing Education Language Institute for their support in the preparation and revision of the text.

Sincere appreciation is also extended to the police officers from the State of Kuwait for their patience and understanding during the testing period of these materials.

The publishers would like to thank the following for permission to reproduce photographs:

Adaptor (Engineering) Ltd.
A.C.T. Sirius
Apple Computer (UK) Ltd.
British Leyland
The Design Council Slide Library
Richard and Sally Greenhill
I.B.M.
I.C.L.
I.T.T. Business Systems
N.C.R. Ltd.
Servis Domestic Appliances
Sinclair Research Ltd.
V.N.U. Business Publications

and the following for their assistance with the cover photograph:

Research Machines Ltd., Oxford
A.C.T. Sirius, courtesy of Oxford Software

Cover photograph by Mark Mason

Contents

About the book 8

PART	SECTION	UNIT/FOCUS
1 The computer	1 Introduction	1 What is a computer? 16 Focus A Contextual reference 21 2 History of computers 23 Focus B Suffixes 29
	2 Description	3 Characteristics 36 Focus C Organizing information 42 4 Computer capabilities and limitations 46 5 Hardware and software 52 Focus D Prefixes 58
	3 Kinds of computers	6 Mainframes 64 Focus E Listing 69 7 Minicomputers 72 8 Microcomputers 77 Focus F Making comparisons 83
2 Computer components	4 The processor	9 The Central Processing Unit 94 Focus G Time sequence 99 10 The Control Unit and the Arithmetic-Logical Unit 102 Focus H Giving examples 107

PART	SECTION	UNIT/FOCUS

2 Computer components	5 Memory	11 Primary and secondary memory *111*
		    Focus I Adding information *116*
		12 Types of memory *119*
		    Focus J Giving an explanation
		    or a definition *124*

	6 Input and output devices	13 Cards and card readers *129*
		    Focus K Classifying *136*
		14 Tapes and tape drives *141*
		15 Disks and disk drives *148*
		    Focus L Contrasting *157*
		16 Printers *160*
		17 Terminals *169*
		    Focus M Cause and effect *176*

3 Data processing	7 Programming	18 Steps in problem solving *186* 19 Computer arithmetic *191* 20 Flowcharting *197* 21 Programs and programming languages *207* Focus N Making predictions *214*
	8 Computer-related topics	22 Time sharing versus batch *218* 23 Careers *224*

Projections *229*

Glossary *231*

About the book

What will students learn from this book?

A growing number of students of computer science and people working with computers have an immediate and specific need to acquire a reading knowledge of computer science *in English*.

To read effectively in a second or foreign language requires both an understanding of the grammar and vocabulary of that language and also the development or application of reading skills. This book helps students in three main ways. Firstly, it provides exercise material on formal aspects of language, such as grammar and vocabulary. The fourteen Focus sections present and practise language functions most readily associated with the English used in computer science: explaining, defining, classifying, predicting, etc. Secondly, it teaches students reading skills such as locating information, finding the main idea of a text, and following the development of an argument. And thirdly, it provides the reader with up-to-date basic information about computers and how they operate, through the subject matter presented in each reading passage. The texts cover a wide range of topics: from the memory to computer arithmetic, from program design to on-line processing.

Who is the book intended for?

English for Computer Science has been written for people who are studying computer science or related subjects in universities, colleges and technical schools, and also for in-company training programs where computer personnel need to improve their understanding of English.

The book can easily be used for self-study by individuals who want to make use of computers privately or for their careers. In this case the accompanying Answer Book will provide the necessary guidance. We would suggest as a study method that the student working alone should always attempt to answer the questions *before* turning to the Answer Book. You can check your answers at the end of each exercise or at the end of a whole unit, but don't be tempted to work with the Answer Book open! Several short study sessions per week are more useful than one long period. Try to do some revision of previous units at least once a week.

If *English for Computer Science* is used purely as a reading course, it should take between 45–60 hours to complete the work, depending, of course, on the students' proficiency in English. However, the book could equally well be used as an integral part of a course which also includes listening, speaking and writing. In that case the course would, necessarily, be considerably longer.

How much computer science must the teacher know?

Since the book is written with the assumption that many readers will have little or no previous knowledge of computer science, it follows that the teacher need not have much technical background in the field. It is advisable, however, that the teacher understands the concepts and terminology introduced in each unit in order to be as much a resource person as possible, to answer queries that may arise in class or at least to direct the students to the appropriate place to find an answer. This type of dialogue and exchange ensures real communication in the classroom, where the students understand that the teacher doesn't have to know everything about computer science but can guide them in finding answers to their questions.

On methodology

Recent concern with defining and establishing purposes for the teaching of English as a foreign language has underlined the importance of reading comprehension as the principle goal in English as a second/foreign language during academic study. In addition, it may be assumed that the native speaker already possesses the language knowledge which permits him or her to learn to distinguish between more and less effective cues and thereby to formulate guesses, ideas and or options as to what the text is about. However, non-native speakers do not always transfer this language knowledge from their own language to the English language, and as a result the teaching of how to read cannot be separated from the teaching of the language itself.

All the exercises that accompany the readings are designed to teach and not to test. These exercises fall into two categories; those that concentrate on form, such as the vocabulary and word formation exercises and those that concentrate on communication, such as the comprehension exercises on the passage – the latter being of utmost importance. Whether these exercises are done at home or in class, it isn't simply the answers in themselves which are important, but how and why these answers were given. In other words, it is the process of reasoning and not just the end result that matters. As an example of this, the students are asked not just whether an answer is 'true' or 'false' but to explain their choice and if necessary to refer to that part of the text that provided them with the information to arrive at their answer. This approach encourages genuine communication among the students or between the students and the teacher, making the classroom student-centered rather than teacher-centered.

We have included various types of exercises in this book, not all of which are used with every text. This is due to the fact that some are more appropriate in developing certain reading skills than others. The use of different exercise types also ensures variety. The reading skills developed are:

a. understanding information directly stated in the text
b. understanding information implied in the text
c. understanding concepts
d. understanding relations between parts of the text through the use of grammatical as well as lexical cohesion devices
e. deducing meaning of new lexical items from context
f. deducing concepts from either directly or indirectly stated information
g. scanning or skimming to locate specific information
h. distinguishing the main ideas from the supporting details
i. selecting important or relevant points to summarize an idea.

The fourteen Focus sections each begin with a presentation and examples of how various language functions operate in English. It is worth taking the students carefully through the presentation phase before they tackle the exercises, even when a particular section is seen as revision of language they already know how to use.

PART 1

The Computer

Computers are electronic machines that process information. They are capable of communicating with the user, of doing five kinds of arithmetic operations, and of making three kinds of decisions. However, they are incapable of thinking. They accept data and instructions as input, and after processing the information, they output the results.

When talking about computers, both hardware and software need to be considered. The former refers to the actual machinery, whereas the latter refers to the programs that control and coordinate the activities of the hardware.

The first computer was built in 1930 but since then computer technology has evolved a great deal. There are three different kinds of computers in use today: the mainframe, the minicomputer, and the microcomputer. All three have one thing in common – they operate quickly and accurately in solving problems.

SECTION 1

Introduction

UNIT 1

What is a computer?

*When you read the following text, you will probably meet words and expressions that are new to you. First try to understand their meaning from the context – read the same passage a few times. When you have read the whole text, check new words in a dictionary. Most of the words in **bold** typeface are explained in the Glossary at the end of this book.*

[1] A computer is a machine with an intricate network of electronic **circuits** that operate **switches** or magnetize tiny metal **cores**. The switches, like the cores, are capable of being in one of two possible states, that is, on or off; magnetized or demagnetized. The machine is capable of storing and manipulating numbers, letters, and characters. The basic idea of a computer is that we can make the machine do what we want by inputting signals that turn certain switches on and turn others off, or that magnetize or do not magnetize the cores.

[2] The basic job of computers is the processing of information. For this reason, computers can be defined as **devices** which accept information in the form of instructions called a **program** and characters called **data**, perform mathematical and/or logical operations on the information, and then supply results of these operations. The program, or part of it, which tells the computers what to do and the data, which provide the information needed to solve the problem, are kept inside the computer in a place called **memory**.

[3] Computers are thought to have many remarkable powers. However, most computers, whether large or small have three basic capabilities. First, computers have circuits for performing arithmetic operations, such as: addition, subtraction, division, multiplication and exponentiation. Second, computers have a means of communicating with the user. After all, if we couldn't feed information in and get results back, these machines wouldn't be of much use. However, certain computers (commonly minicomputers and microcomputers) are used to control directly things such as robots, aircraft navigation systems, medical instruments, etc.

[4] Some of the most common methods of inputting information are to use **punched cards, magnetic tape, disks,** and **terminals.** The computer's **input device** (which might be a **card reader,** a **tape drive** or **disk drive,**

depending on the **medium** used in inputting information) reads the information into the computer.

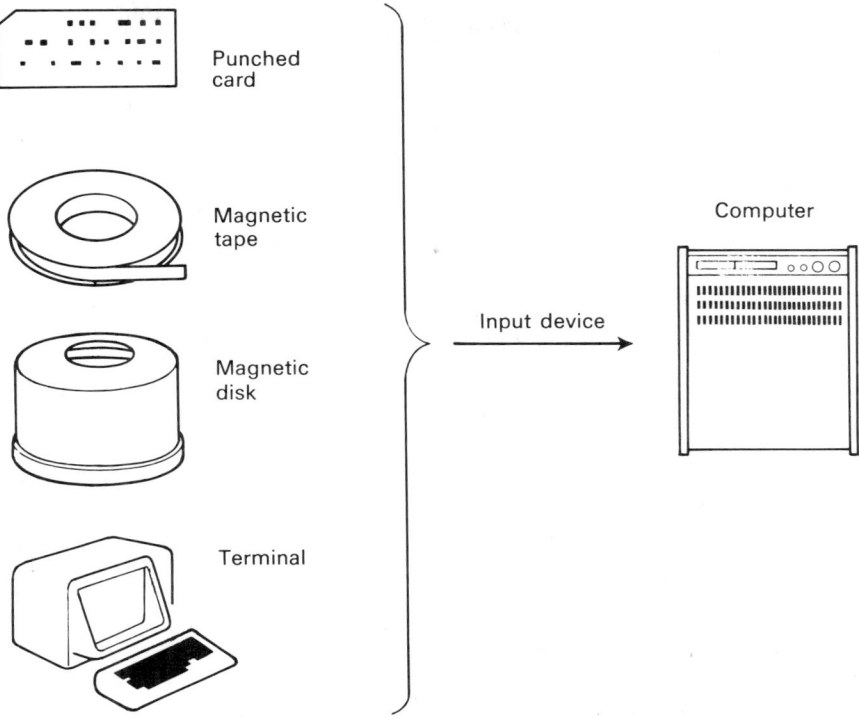

For outputting information, two common devices used are a printer which prints the new information on paper, or a **CRT display screen** which shows the results on a TV-like screen.

[5] Third, computers have circuits which can make decisions. The kinds of decisions which computer circuits can make are not of the type: 'Who would win a war between two countries?' or 'Who is the richest person in the world?' Unfortunately, the computer can only decide three things, namely: Is one number less than another? Are two numbers equal? and, Is one number greater than another?

[6] A computer can solve a series of problems and make hundreds, even thousands, of logical decisions without becoming tired or bored. It can find the solution to a problem in a fraction of the time it takes a human being to do the job. A computer can replace people in dull, routine tasks, but it has no originality; it works according to the **instructions** given to it and cannot exercise any value judgments. There are times when a computer seems to operate like a mechanical 'brain', but its achievements are limited by the minds of human beings. A computer cannot do anything unless a person tells it what to do and gives it the appropriate information; but because electric pulses can move at the

speed of light, a computer can carry out vast numbers of arithmetic-logical operations almost instantaneously. A person can do everything a computer can do, but in many cases that person would be dead long before the job was finished.

Exercises

1 Main idea

Which statement best expresses the main idea of the text? Why did you eliminate the other choices?

☐ 1. Computers have changed the way in which many kinds of jobs are done.

☐ 2. Instructions and data must be given to the computer to act on.

☐ 3. Computers are machines capable of processing and outputting data.

☐ 4. Without computers, many tasks would take much longer to do.

2 Understanding the passage

Decide whether the following statements are true or false (T/F) by referring to the information in the text. Then make the necessary changes so that the false statements become true.

T   F

☐ ☐ 1. A computer can store or handle any data even if it hasn't received information to do so.

☐ ☐ 2. All computers accept and process information in the form of instructions and characters.

☐ ☐ 3. The information necessary for solving problems is found in the memory of the computer.

☐ ☐ 4. Not all computers can perform arithmetic operations, make decisions, and communicate in some way with the user.

☐ ☐ 5. Computers can still be useful machines even if they can't communicate with the user.

☐ ☐ 6. There are many different devices used for feeding information into a computer.

☐ ☐ 7. There aren't as many different types of devices used for giving results as there are for accepting information.

Unit 1 What is a computer?

T	F	
☐	☐	8. Computers can make any type of decision they are asked to.
☐	☐	9. Computers can work endlessly without having to stop to rest unless there is a breakdown.

3 Locating information

Find the passages in the text where the following ideas are expressed. Give line references as in the example below.

ll. 10–13   1. Computers accept information, perform mathematical and/or logical operations then supply new information.
.... 2. All computers have three basic capabilities.
.... 3. A computer is a machine that can be made to operate by receiving signals.
.... 4. A computer cannot work without being told what to do.
.... 5. A computer can make three types of decisions.
.... 6. The fundamental job of a computer is processing information.
.... 7. A computer can do the work of hundreds of people in a very short time.
.... 8. The memory of a computer is used for storing information.

4 Understanding words

Refer back to the text and find synonyms (i.e. words with a similar meaning) for the following words.

1. complex   (*l. 1*)   *intricate* ....
2. fundamental   (*l. 9*)   ....
3. a way   (*l. 21*)   ....
4. uninterested   (*l. 42*)   ....
5. accomplishments   (*l. 48*)   ....

Now refer back to the text and find antonyms (i.e. words with an opposite meaning) for the following words.

6. large   (*l. 2*)   *tiny* ....
7. receiving   (*l. 7*)   ....
8. reject   (*l. 10*)   ....
9. unusual   (*l. 27*)   ....
10. small   (*l. 51*)   ....

5 Content review

Try to think of a definition for each of these items before checking them in the Glossary. Then complete the following statements with the appropriate words. (Some can be used more than once.) Make sure you use the correct form, i.e. singular or plural.

core	device	data
circuit	terminal	switch
program	memory	medium
CRT display		

1. Every computer has *circuits* for performing arithmetic operations, operating .... or magnetized ....

2. A .... with a screen is normally referred to as a .... unit.

3. A computer is a .... that processes information in the form of .... and .... and can store this information in a ....

4. Card readers, tape drives, or disk drives are different .... for inputting information.

FOCUS A

Contextual reference

Transitional markers are words used to link ideas together so that the text is smoother to read. When pronouns such as **it, they, them, I, he, she, which, who, whose, that, such, one,** and demonstrative adjectives such as **this, that, these** and **those,** are used as transitional markers, they refer to a word, or words, mentioned earlier in the sentence or paragraph. Their function is to take your thoughts back to something that has already been mentioned. Thus they serve as synonyms or substitutes. Other words which are often used to refer backwards are **the former, the latter, the first, second, etc., the last.**

Sample paragraph

A computer like any other machine, is used because it does certain jobs better and more efficiently than humans. It can receive more information and process it faster than any human. The speed at which a computer works can replace weeks or even months of pencil-and-paper work. Therefore, computers are used when the time saved offsets their cost which is one of the many reasons they are used so much in business, industry and research.

Exercise 1

Using the sample paragraph as a model, draw a rectangle around the word, or words, that the circled words refer to. Then join the ○ and the ▢ with arrows.

Computers are electronic machines that process information. They are capable of communicating with the user, of doing different kinds of arithmetic operations and of making three kinds of decisions. However, they are incapable of thinking. They accept data and instructions as input, and after processing it they output the results.

When talking about computers, both hardware and software need to be considered. The (former) refers to the actual machinery, whereas the latter refers to the programs (which) control and coordinate the activities of the hardware while processing the data.

The first computer was built in 1930 but since then computer technology has evolved a great deal. There are three different kinds of computers in use today: the mainframe, the minicomputer and the microcomputer. (These) all have one thing in common: (they) operate quickly and accurately in solving problems.

Exercise 2
Now look back at the text 'What Is a Computer?' and find out what the words in **bold** typeface refer to.

1. **that** operate switches (l. 2) *electronic circuits*
2. **which** accept information (l. 10) ....
3. or part of **it** (l. 13) ....
4. **which** tells the computers (l. 14) ....
5. **which** prints the new information (l. 33) ....
6. **which** shows the results (l. 34) ....
7. **which** can make decisions (l. 35) ....
8. **It** can find the solution (l. 42) ....
9. **it** has no originality (l. 45) ....
10. tells **it** what to do (l. 49) ....

UNIT 2

History of computers

*When you read the following text, you will probably meet words and expressions that are new to you. First try to understand their meaning from the context – read the same passage a few times. When you have read the whole text, check new words in a dictionary. Most of the words in **bold** typeface are explained in the Glossary at the end of this book.*

[1] Let us take a look at the history of the computers that we know today. The very first calculating device used was the ten fingers of a man's hands. This, in fact, is why today we still count in tens and multiples of tens. Then the **abacus** was invented, a bead frame in which the beads are moved from left to right. People went on using some form of abacus well into the 16th century, and it is still being used in some parts of the world because it can be understood without knowing how to read.

[2] During the 17th and 18th centuries many people tried to find easy ways of calculating. J. Napier, a Scotsman, devised a mechanical way of multiplying and dividing, which is how the modern **slide rule** works. Henry Briggs used Napier's ideas to produce **logarithm tables** which all mathematicians use today. **Calculus,** another branch of mathematics, was independently invented by both Sir Isaac Newton, an Englishman, and Leibnitz, a German mathematician.

[3] The first real calculating machine appeared in 1820 as the result of several people's experiments. This type of machine, which saves a great deal of time and reduces the possibility of making mistakes, depends on a series of ten-toothed gear wheels. In 1830 Charles Babbage, an Englishman, designed a machine that was called 'The Analytical Engine'. This machine, which Babbage showed at the Paris Exhibition in 1855, was an attempt to cut out the human being altogether, except for providing the machine with the necessary facts about the problem to be solved. He never finished this work, but many of his ideas were the basis for building today's computers.

[4] In 1930, the first **analog** computer was built by an American named Vannevar Bush. This device was used in World War II to help aim guns. Mark I, the name given to the first **digital** computer, was completed in 1944. The men responsible for this invention were Professor Howard Aiken and some people from IBM. This was the first

machine that could figure out long lists of mathematical problems, all at a very fast rate. In 1946 two engineers at the University of Pennsylvania, J. Eckert and J. Mauchly, built the first digital computer using parts called **vacuum tubes**. They named their new invention ENIAC. Another important advancement in computers came in 1947, when John von Newmann developed the idea of keeping instructions for the computer inside the computer's memory.

[5] The first generation of computers, which used vacuum tubes, came out in 1950. Univac I is an example of these computers which could perform thousands of calculations per second. In 1960, the second generation of computers was developed and these could perform work ten times faster than their predecessors. The reason for this extra speed was the use of **transistors** instead of vacuum tubes. Second-generation computers were smaller, faster and more dependable than first-generation computers. The third-generation computers appeared on the market in 1965. These computers could do a million calculations a second, which is 1000 times as many as first-generation computers. Unlike second-generation computers, these are controlled by tiny integrated circuits and are consequently smaller and more dependable. Fourth-generation computers have now arrived, and the integrated circuits that are being developed have been greatly reduced in size. This is due to **microminiaturization**, which means that the circuits are much smaller than before; as many as 1000 tiny circuits now fit onto a single **chip**. A chip is a square or rectangular piece of silicon, usually from $\frac{1}{10}$ to $\frac{1}{4}$ inch, upon which several layers of an integrated circuit are etched or imprinted, after which the circuit is encapsulated in plastic, ceramic or metal. Fourth-generation computers are 50 times faster than third-generation computers and can complete approximately 1,000,000 instructions per second.

[6] At the rate computer technology is growing, today's computers might be obsolete by 1985 and most certainly by 1990. It has been said that if transport technology had developed as rapidly as computer technology, a trip across the Atlantic Ocean today would take a few seconds.

Exercises

1 Main idea
Which statement best expresses the main idea of the text? Why did you eliminate the other choices?

☐ 1. Computers, as we know them today, have gone through many changes.

☐ 2. Today's computer probably won't be around for long.

☐ 3. Computers have had a very short history.

Unit 2 History of computers

2 Understanding the passage

Decide whether the following statements are true or false (T/F) by referring to the information in the text. Then make the necessary changes so that the false statements become true.

T F

1. The abacus and the fingers are two calculating devices still in use today.
2. The slide rule was invented hundreds of years ago.
3. During the early 1880s, many people worked on inventing a mechanical calculating machine.
4. Charles Babbage, an Englishman, could well be called the father of computers.
5. The first computer was invented and built in the USA.
6. Instructions used by computers have always been kept inside the computer's memory.
7. Using transistors instead of vacuum tubes did nothing to increase the speed at which calculations were done.
8. As computers evolved, their size decreased and their dependability increased.
9. Today's computers have more circuits than previous computers.
10. Computer technology has developed to a point from which new developments in the field will take a long time to come.

3 Locating information

Find the passages in the text where the following ideas are expressed. Give the line references.

.... 1. During the same period in history, logarithm tables and calculus were developed.
.... 2. It wasn't until the 19th century that a calculating machine was invented which tried to reduce manpower.
.... 3. Integrated circuitry has further changed computers.
.... 4. People used their fingers to count.
.... 5. The computers of the future may be quite different from those in use today.
.... 6. Today's computer circuits can be put on a chip.
.... 7. Then an instrument with beads was invented for counting before a mechanical way for multiplying and dividing was devised.
.... 8. Transistors replaced vacuum tubes.

4 Understanding words

Refer back to the text and find synonyms (i.e. words with a similar meaning) for the following words.

1. machine   (l. 2)   ....
2. designed   (l. 9)   ....
3. a lot   (l. 16)   ....
4. errors   (l. 17)   ....
5. solve   (l. 30)   ....

Now refer back to the text and find antonyms (i.e. words with an opposite meaning) for the following words.

6. old   (l. 10) ....
7. a few   (l. 16) ....
8. to include   (l. 21) ....
9. contemporaries (l. 41) ....
10. still in use   (l. 60) ....

5a Content review

Match the following words in column A with the statements in column B. The first one is done for you.

	A		B
c	1. abacus	a.	instrument used for doing multiplication and division
☐	2. calculus	b.	used in the first digital computers
☐	3. analog computer	c.	an instrument used for counting
☐	4. digital computer	d.	used in mathematics
☐	5. vacuum tubes	e.	circuitry of fourth-generation computers
☐	6. transistors	f.	invented by Americans in 1944
☐	7. chip	g.	made computers smaller and faster
☐	8. microminiaturization	h.	used to help aim guns
☐	9. slide rule	i.	the reduction of circuitry onto a chip
☐	10. logarithm tables	j.	a branch of mathematics

Unit 2 History of computers

5b Content review

Use the information in the text on 'History of Computers' to complete the following table.

TIME	EVENT
Primitive times	
	Abacus invented
17th and 18th centuries	
	Henry Briggs produced logarithm tables
	Charles Babbage designed
1930	
	First use of in
1947	
	Second-generation computers using
Now	
Future	

6 Focus review

Focus A   Contextual reference

Now look back at the text 'History of Computers' and find out what the words in **bold** typeface refer to.

1. **that** we know today (*l. 1*) ....
2. and **it** is still being used (*l. 6*) ....
3. **which** all mathematicians use today (*l. 11*) ....
4. **which** saves a great deal of time (*l. 16*) ....
5. **that** was called 'The Analytical Engine' (*l. 19*) ....
6. **that** could figure out long lists (*l. 30*) ....
7. **They** named their new invention (*l. 33*) ....
8. **which** could perform (*l. 38*) ....
9. and **these** could perform (*l. 40*) ....
10. **that** are being developed (*l. 50*) ....

FOCUS B

Word formation – Suffixes

When you are reading, you will come across unfamiliar words. It is often possible to guess the meanings of these words if you understand the way words in English are generally formed.

An English word can be divided into three parts: a prefix, a stem and a suffix. *Pre-* means 'before'; a *prefix*, therefore, is what comes before the stem. Consider as an example, the prefix **de-** (meaning 'reduce' or 'reverse') in a word like **de**magnetize (meaning 'to deprive of magnetism'). A *suffix* is what is attached to the end of the stem. Consider as an example the suffix **-er** (meaning 'someone who') in programm**er** ('the person who programs'). Both prefixes and suffixes are referred to as *affixes*.

Prefixes usually change the meaning of the word; for example, **un-** changes a word to the negative. **Un**magnetizable means 'not capable of being magnetized'. Suffixes, on the other hand, change the word from one part of speech to another. For example, **-ly** added to the adjective quick gives the adverb quick**ly**. Let us now consider some suffixes and their usual meanings.

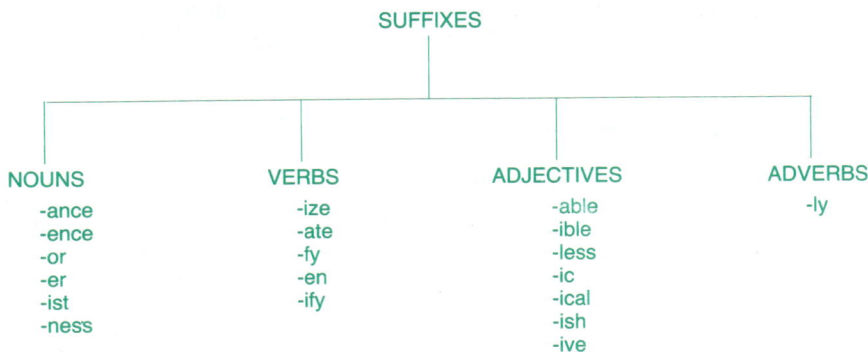

Exercise 1

Study these tables and try to find additional examples. Use your dictionary if necessary.

Noun-forming suffixes

SUFFIX	MEANING	EXAMPLES
-ance	state	performance
-ence	quality of	independence
-er, -or	a person who / a thing which	programmer, operator / compiler, accumulator
-ation / -tion	the act of	execution
-ist / -yst	a person who	analyst, typist
-ness	condition of	cleanliness
-ion	action/state	conversion
-ing	activity	multiplexing
-ment	state, action	measurement
-ity	state, quality	electricity
-ian	pertaining to	electrician
-ism	condition/state	magnetism
-dom	domain/condition	freedom
-ship	condition/state	relationship, partnership, friendship
-ary		binary

Verb-forming suffixes

SUFFIX	MEANING	EXAMPLES
-ize	to make	computerize
-ate		automate, activate, calculate
-fy		simplify
-en		harden, widen

Adverb-forming suffix

SUFFIX	MEANING	EXAMPLES
-ly	in the manner of	electronically, logically, comparably, helpfully

Focus B Word formation – Suffixes

Adjective-forming suffixes		
SUFFIX	MEANING	EXAMPLES
-al -ar -ic -ical	have the quality of	computational, logical circular magnetic, automatic electrical
-able -ible	capable of being	comparable divisible
-ous -ious	like, full of	dangerous religious
-ful	characterized by	helpful
-less	without	careless
-ish	like	yellowish
-ed	having	computed, punched
-ive	quality of	interactive
-ing	to make or do	programming, coding, processing, multiplexing

Exercise 2

Read the following sentences and underline all the suffixes. Then try to find out what parts of speech the words are.

1. The systems analyst provides the programmer with the details of the data processing problems.
2. CRT terminals are very useful interactive devices for use in offices because of their speed and quietness.
3. The new microcomputer we purchased does not have a Fortran compiler. It is programmable in Basic only.
4. A computer is a machine with an intricate network of electronic circuits that operate switches or magnetize tiny metal cores.
5. In very large and modern installations, the computer operator sits in front of a screen that shows an up-to-date summary of the computer jobs as they are being processed.
6. The introduction of terminals and screens has partly replaced the use of punched cards.
7. Binary arithmetic is based on two digits: 0 and 1.
8. Multiplexing is when many electrical signals are combined and carried on only one optical link.
9. Computers are machines designed to process electronically specially prepared pieces of information.
10. The computed results were printed in tables.

Exercise 3

Some forms of the words in 1–5 below were used in the text 'What Is a Computer?' (Unit 1).

Fill in each blank with the appropriate form of the words.

1. operation, operate, operator, operational, operationally, operating
   a. A computer can perform mathematical .... very quickly.
   b. One of the first persons to note that the computer is malfunctioning is the computer ....
   c. The job of a computer operator is to .... the various machines in a computer installation.
   d. The new machines in the computer installation are not yet ....

2. acceptance, accept, accepted, acceptable, acceptably
   a. A computer is a device which .... processes and gives out information.
   b. The students are still waiting for their .... into the Computer Science program.
   c. It is .... to work without a template if the flowcharts are not kept on file.

3. solution, solve, solvable, solver
   a. It may take a lot of time to find a .... to a complex problem in programming.
   b. A computer can .... a problem faster than any human being.
   c. A computer has often been referred to as a problem ....

4. remark, remarkable, remarkably, remarked
   a. Today's computers are .... faster than their predecessors.
   b. Systems analysts will often make .... about existing programs so as to help make the operations more efficient.
   c. There have been .... developments in the field of computer science in the last decade.

5. communication, communicate, communicable, communicative, communicably
   a. A computer must be able to .... with the user.

Focus B Word formation – Suffixes

  b. Fibre optics is a new development in the field of ....

  c. Some people working in computer installations aren't very .... because they are shy.

Some forms of the words in 6–10 below were used in the text 'History of Computers' (Unit 2).

Fill in each blank with the appropriate form of the words.

6. calculation, calculate, calculating, calculated, calculator, calculable, calculus

  a. A computer can do many kinds of .... quickly and accurately.

  b. .... is a branch of mathematics for making .... without the use of a .... machine.

  c. A computer can .... numbers much faster than a manual ....

  d. Some problems aren't .... without logarithm tables.

7. mechanic, mechanism, mechanize, mechanical, mechanically, mechanistic, mechanics, mechanization, mechanized

  a. Today's computers are less .... than they used to be.

  b. The .... devices in a computer system operate more slowly than the electromagnetic devices.

  c. The .... of the brain is very complicated but unlike a computer it isn't ....

8. necessity, necessitate, necessary, necessarily, necessities, need, needed

  a. Because it is expensive to set up a computer department it is .... to budget well for the basic .... of the installations.

  b. A good programmer isn't .... going to be a good systems analyst.

  c. Students' lack of understanding of the basic concepts in computer science may .... the instructor to restructure the course.

9. dependence, depend on, dependable, dependably, dependent, dependency, depending
   a. The length of time a programmer takes to make a program will vary .... on the complexity of the problem and his ability and experience.
   b. One can always .... a computer to obtain accurate answers because it's probably the most .... machine in the world today.

10. technology, technological, technologically, technologist
    a. Computer .... is a fast growing discipline.
    b. The .... improvements of computers are reducing man's workload.

SECTION 2
Description

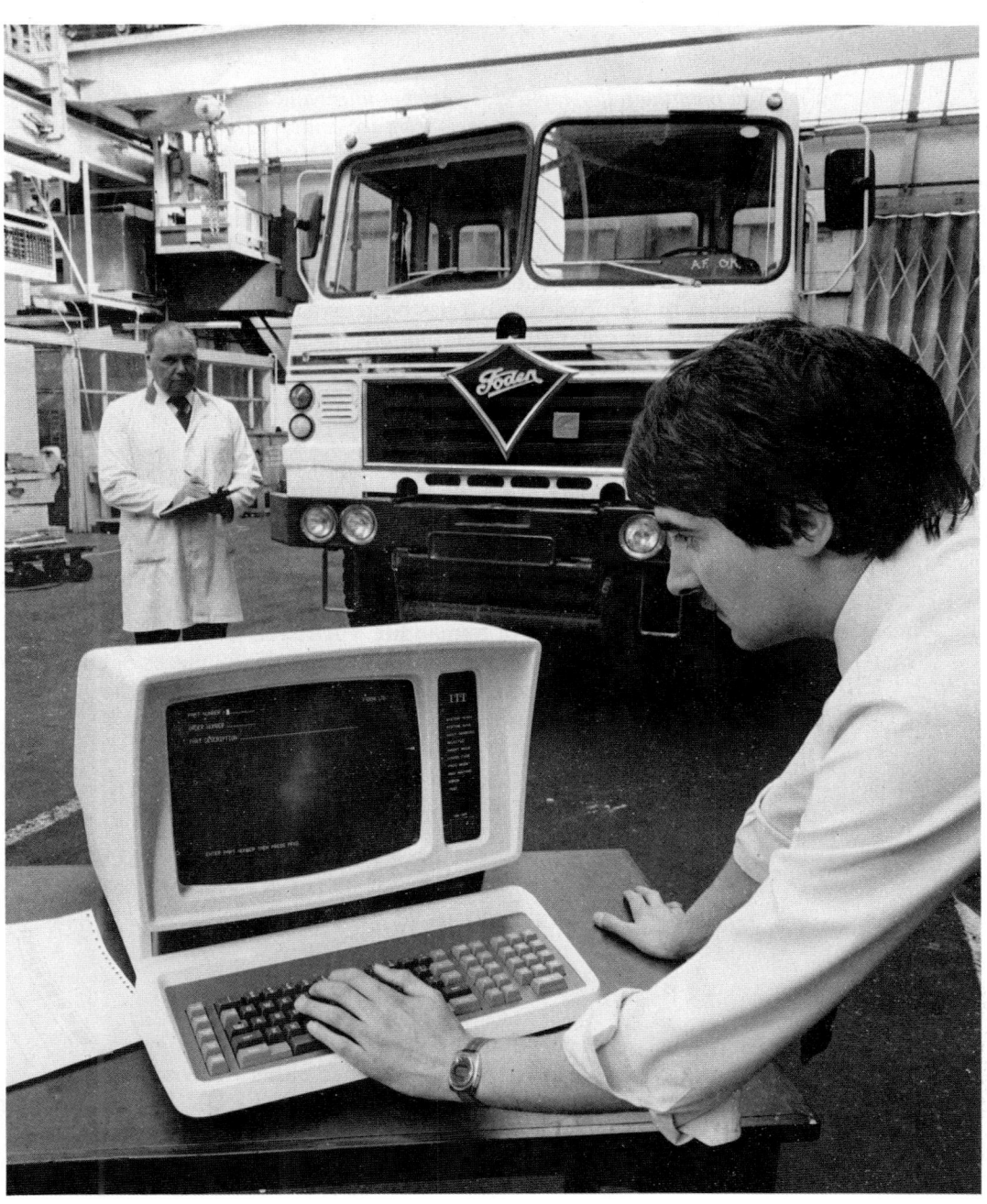

UNIT 3

Characteristics

*When you read the following text, remember to try and understand the meaning of new words and expressions from the context. Don't check new words in the dictionary until you have read the whole text. Most of the words in **bold** typeface are explained in the Glossary at the end of the book.*

[1] Computers are machines designed to process, electronically, specially prepared pieces of information which are termed data. Handling or manipulating the information that has been given to the computer, in such ways as doing calculations, adding information or making comparisons is called **processing**. Computers are made up of millions of electronic devices capable of storing data or moving them, at enormous speeds, through complex circuits with different functions.

[2] All computers have several characteristics in common, regardless of make or design. Information, in the form of instructions and data, is given to the machine, after which the machine acts on it, and a result is then returned. The information presented to the machine is the **input**; the internal manipulative operations, the **processing**; and the result, the **output**. These three basic concepts of input, processing, and output occur in almost every aspect of human life whether at work or at play. For example, in clothing manufacturing, the input is the pieces of cut cloth, the processing is the sewing together of these pieces, and the output is the finished garment.

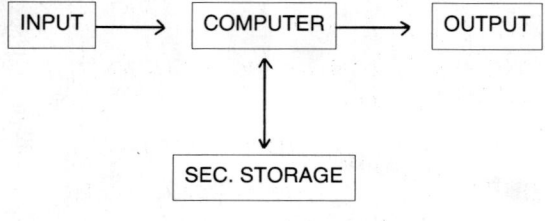

Figure 3.1

[3] Figure 3.1 shows schematically the fundamental hardware components in a computer system. The centerpiece is called either the computer, the **processor**, or, usually, the **central processing unit** (**CPU**). The term 'computer' includes those parts of **hardware** in which calculations and

other data manipulations are performed, and the high-speed internal memory in which data and calculations are stored during actual execution of programs. Attached to the CPU are the various **peripheral devices** such as card readers and **keyboards** (two common examples of input devices). When data or programs need to be saved for long periods of time, they are stored on various **secondary memory** devices or **storage devices** such as magnetic tapes or magnetic disks.

[4] Computers have often been thought of as extremely large adding machines, but this is a very narrow view of their function. Although a computer can only respond to a certain number of instructions, it is not a **single-purpose** machine since these instructions can be combined in an infinite number of sequences. Therefore, a computer has no known limit on the kinds of things it can do; its versatility is limited only by the imagination of those using it.

[5] In the late 1950s and early 1960s when electronic computers of the kind in use today were being developed, they were very expensive to own and run. Moreover, their size and reliability were such that a large number of support personnel were needed to keep the equipment operating. This has all changed now that computing power has become portable, more compact, and cheaper.

[6] In only a very short period of time, computers have greatly changed the way in which many kinds of work are performed. Computers can remove many of the routine and boring tasks from our lives, thereby leaving us with more time for interesting, creative work. It goes without saying that computers have created whole new areas of work that did not exist before their development.

Exercises

1 Main idea

Which statement or statements best express the main idea of the text? Why did you eliminate the other choices?

☐ 1. Computers have changed the way in which we live.

☐ 2. All computers have an input, a processor, an output and a storage device.

☐ 3. Computers have decreased man's workload.

☐ 4. All computers have the same basic hardware components.

2 Understanding the passage

Decide whether the following statements are true or false (T/F) by referring to the information in the text. Then, make the necessary changes so that the false statements become true.

T F

☐ ☐ 1. All information to be processed must be prepared in such a way that the computer will understand it.

☐ ☐ 2. Because of the complex electronic circuitry of a computer, data can be either stored or moved about at high speeds.

☐ ☐ 3. Not all computers can process data given to them and produce results.

☐ ☐ 4. The basic concepts of data processing are restricted to computers alone.

☐ ☐ 5. The processor is the central component of a computer system.

☐ ☐ 6. All other devices used in a computer system are attached to the CPU.

☐ ☐ 7. Memory devices are used for storing information.

☐ ☐ 8. Computers are very much restricted in what they can do.

☐ ☐ 9. Computers today cost less, are smaller, and need fewer people to operate them than in the past.

☐ ☐ 10. Computers haven't changed our working conditions very much.

3 Locating information

Find the passages in the text where the following ideas are expressed. Give the line references.

.... 1. All computers are basically the same.
.... 2. Then arithmetic and/or decision-making operations are performed.
.... 3. Computers are limited by man's imagination more than anything else.
.... 4. All the equipment used in a computer system is the hardware.
.... 5. Computers are electronic machines used for processing data.

Unit 3 Characteristics

.... 6. If programs or data need to be kept for a long time, they are stored on tapes or disks.
.... 7. First the computer accepts data.
.... 8. Finally, new information is presented to the user.

4 Contextual reference

Look back at the text and find out what the words in **bold** typeface refer to.

1. **which** are termed data (l. 2) ....
2. or moving **them** (l. 6) ....
3. the machine acts on **it** (l. 10) ....
4. **they** are stored on (l. 27) ....
5. **it** is not a single-purpose machine (l. 31) ....
6. the kinds of things **it** can do (l. 34) ....
7. of those using **it** (l. 35) ....
8. **they** were very expensive to own (l. 37) ....
9. Moreover, **their** size and reliability (l. 38) ....
10. **that** did not exist (l. 46) ....

5 Understanding words

Refer back to the text and find synonyms (i.e. words with a similar meaning) for the following words.

1. called (l. 2) ....
2. tremendous (l. 6) ....
3. ideas (l. 13) ....
4. react (l. 31) ....
5. take away (l. 44) ....

Now refer back to the text and find antonyms (i.e. words with an opposite meaning) for the following words.

6. taken away (l. 11) ....
7. wide (l. 30) ....
8. limited (l. 33) ....
9. immovable (l. 40) ....
10. after (l. 47) ....

6 Word forms

First choose the appropriate form of the words to complete the sentences. Then check the differences of meaning in your dictionary.

1. imagination, imagine, imaginable, imaginative, imaginary
   a. A computer is limited in its ability by the .... of man.
   b. Some people are good at inventing .... stories.
   c. It is practically impossible to .... the speed at which a computer calculates numbers.

2. addition, add, added, additional, additionally, additive
   a. Many terminals can be .... to a basic system if the need arises.
   b. .... and subtraction are two basic mathematical operations.
   c. When buying a system there is often no .... charge for the programs.

3. complication, complicate, complicated, complicating, complicatedly
   a. There can be many .... involved in setting up a computer in an old building.
   b. It is sometimes a very .... process getting into a computer installation for security reasons.
   c. It is sometimes very .... to explain computer concepts.

4. difference, differ, different, differently, differential, differentiate
   a. There isn't a very big .... in flowcharting for a program to be written in Cobol or Fortran.
   b. There are many .... computer manufacturers today, and a buyer must be able to .... between the advantages and disadvantages of each.
   c. The opinions of programmers as to the best way of solving a problem often .... greatly.

5. reliably, rely on, reliable, reliability
   a. Computers are .... machines.
   b. If you don't know the meaning of a computer term, you cannot always .... an all-purpose dictionary for the answer.
   c. Computers can do mathematical operations quickly and ....

7a Content review

Try to think of a definition for each of these items before checking them in the Glossary. Then complete the following statements with the appropriate words. (Some can be used more than once.) Make sure you use the correct form, i.e. singular or plural.

processing	hardware	magnetic tape
input	processor	magnetic disk
output	secondary memory	personnel
single-purpose		

1. Information .... takes place in the .... not in the .... device or .... device.
2. The .... refers to all the electromechanical devices used in a computer installation.
3. .... and .... units are used as .... storage devices.
4. A computer isn't usually a .... machine and may require quite specialized .... to operate it and all its related equipment.

7b Content review

Summarize the text on 'Characteristics' by completing the following table.

SYSTEM	COMPONENTS	PARTS
Hardware		1.
		2. *Control Unit*
		3.
	Peripheral devices *A.*	1.
		2. *Disks*
	B. others	3.
		4.
		5.
		6.

FOCUS C

Organizing information

A paragraph is a group of related sentences that develop an idea. In nearly every paragraph, there is one idea that is more important than all the others. This idea is called the *main idea* of the paragraph and is usually found at the beginning of the paragraph.

Sample paragraph 1
All computers, whether large or small, have the same basic capabilities. They have circuits for performing arithmetic operations. They all have a way of communicating with the person(s) using them. They also have circuits for making decisions.

In sample paragraph 1, the first sentence, '**All computers, whether large or small, have the same basic capabilities.**' expresses the *main idea* of the paragraph.

All main idea sentences have a *topic* and say something *about the topic*.

Example
All computers,   [*topic*]   whether large or small, **have the same basic capabilities.**   [*about the topic*]

In some of your reading, finding main ideas may serve your needs but in much of your studying you need to grasp *details*. It is sometimes more difficult to grasp and understand details than main ideas. You will find it helpful if you think of details as growing out of the main idea. In sample paragraph 1, there are three *major details* growing out of the main idea. These are the major details:

1. They have circuits for **performing arithmetic operations**.
2. They all have a way of **communicating with the person(s) using them**.
3. They also have circuits for **making decisions**.

A major detail often has *minor details* growing out of it. These minor details tell more about a major detail, just as major details tell more about a main idea. In studying, you often find a paragraph that has many small details that you must grasp and remember. Breaking up a

Focus C Organizing information

paragraph of this kind into its three components: the *main idea*, *major details* and *minor details* will help you to understand and remember what it is about.

Sample paragraph 2

It is the incredible speed of computers along with their memory capacity that make them so useful and valuable. Computers can solve problems in a fraction of the time it takes man. For this reason, businesses use them to keep their accounts, and airlines, trainlines and buslines use them to keep track of ticket sales. As for memory, modern computers can store information with high accuracy and reliability. A computer can put data into its 'memory' and retrieve it again in a few millionths of a second. It also has a storage capacity for as many as a million items.

If you were to organize this paragraph into its three components, it would look like this:

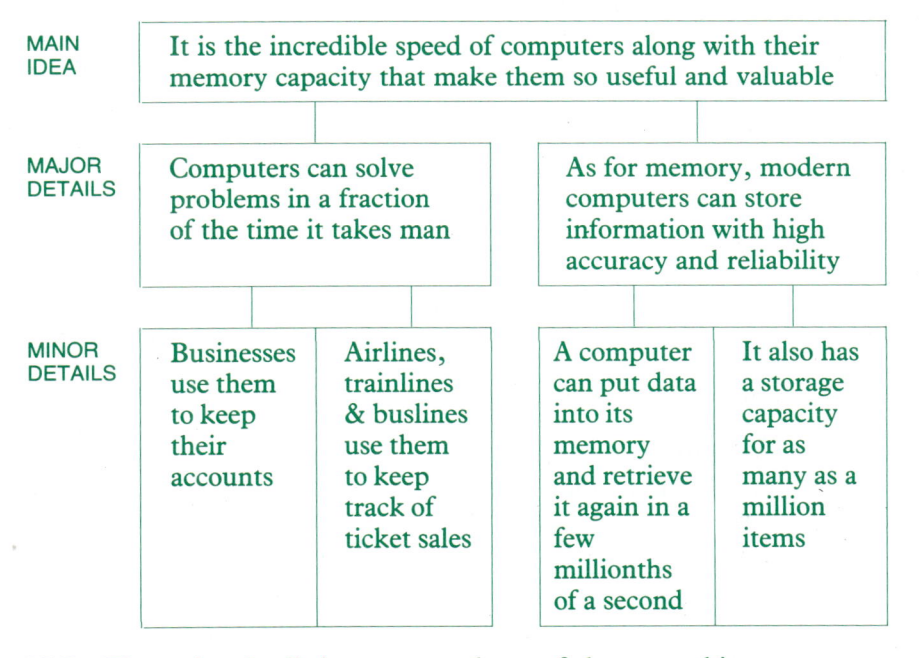

MAIN IDEA	It is the incredible speed of computers along with their memory capacity that make them so useful and valuable			
MAJOR DETAILS	Computers can solve problems in a fraction of the time it takes man		As for memory, modern computers can store information with high accuracy and reliability	
MINOR DETAILS	Businesses use them to keep their accounts	Airlines, trainlines & buslines use them to keep track of ticket sales	A computer can put data into its memory and retrieve it again in a few millionths of a second	It also has a storage capacity for as many as a million items

N.B. The major details in a paragraph are of about equal importance. Because minor details grow out of major details and also give information about major details, they are less important.

In making a block diagram you don't have to write every word in the main idea sentence or in each of the detail sentences.

Exercise 1

Practise finding the *main idea*, *major details* and *minor details* by completing the block diagram after reading the following paragraph.

The computer has changed the production of copy in the newspaper industry. There are three steps involved in the process: input, correction and output. First, the computer numbers each story, counts words and gives a listing of the length of each story. Then a page is made up, advertisements are placed in, the copy is shifted or deleted and corrections are made. Finally, the computer hyphenates words and the result of all this is a newspaper page.

MAIN IDEA	*The computer has changed the production of copy in the newspaper industry.*

MAJOR DETAILS	

MINOR DETAILS			

Exercise 2

Practise finding the *main idea*, *major details* and *minor details* by completing the diagram after reading the following paragraph.

Railways use large computer systems to control ticket reservations and to give immediate information on the status of its trains. The computer system is connected by private telephone lines to terminals in major train stations and ticket reservations for customers are made through these. The passenger's name, type of accommodation and the train schedule is put into the computer's memory. On a typical day, a railway's computer system gets thousands of telephone calls about reservations, space on other railways, and requests for arrivals and departures. A big advantage of the railway computer ticket reservation system is its rapidity because a cancelled booking can be sold anywhere in the system just a few seconds later. Railway computer systems are not used for reservations alone. They are used for a variety of other jobs including train schedules, planning, freight and cargo loading, meal planning, personnel availability, accounting and stock control.

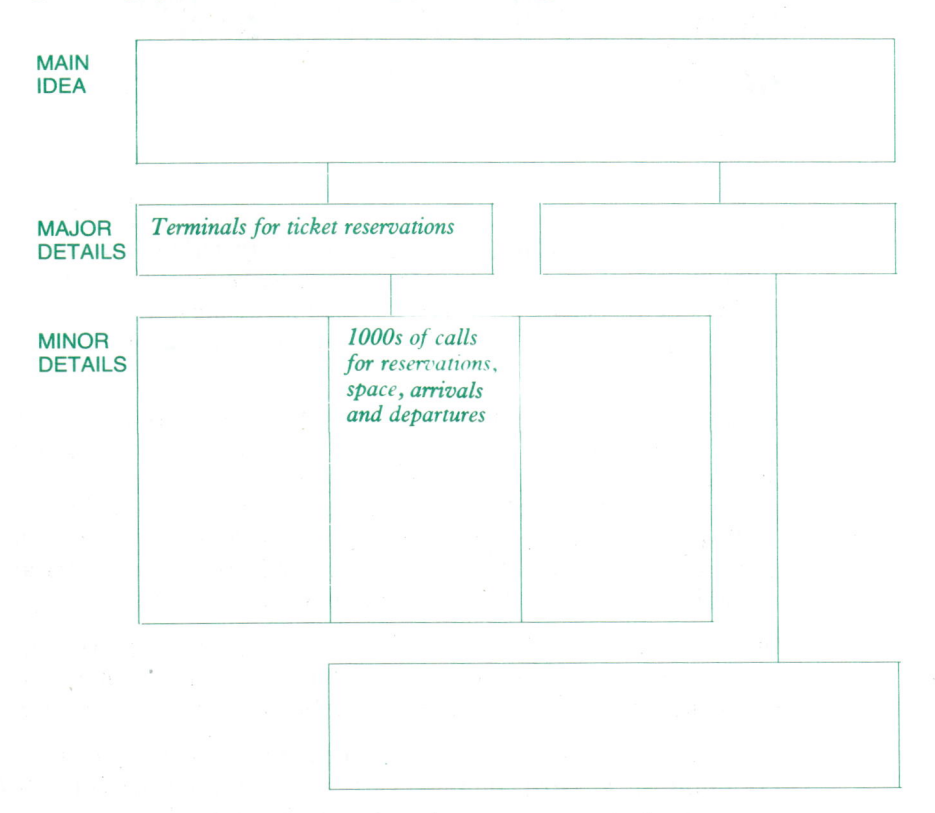

MAIN IDEA

MAJOR DETAILS — *Terminals for ticket reservations*

MINOR DETAILS — *1000s of calls for reservations, space, arrivals and departures*

UNIT 4

Computer capabilities and limitations

*When you read the following text remember to try and understand the meaning of new words and expressions from the context. Don't check new words in the dictionary until you have read the whole text. Most of the words in **bold** typeface are explained in the Glossary at the end of the book.*

[1] Like all machines, a computer needs to be directed and controlled in order to perform a task successfully. Until such time as a program is prepared and stored in the computer's memory, the computer 'knows' absolutely nothing, not even how to accept or reject data. Even the most sophisticated computer, no matter how capable it is, must be told what to do. Until the **capabilities** and the **limitations** of a computer are recognized, its usefulness cannot be thoroughly understood.

[2] In the first place, it should be recognized that computers are capable of doing repetitive operations. A computer can perform similar operations thousands of times, without becoming bored, tired, or even careless.

[3] Secondly, computers can process information at extremely rapid rates. For example, modern computers can solve certain classes of arithmetic problems millions of times faster than a skilled mathematician. Speeds for performing **decision-making** operations are comparable to those for arithmetic operations but input-output operations, however, involve mechanical motion and hence require more time. On a typical **computer system,** cards are read at an average speed of 1000 cards per minute and as many as 1000 lines can be printed at the same rate.

[4] Thirdly, computers may be programmed to calculate answers to whatever level of accuracy is specified by the **programmer**. In spite of newspaper headlines such as 'Computer Fails', these machines are very accurate and reliable especially when the number of operations they can perform every second is considered. Because they are man-made machines, they sometimes malfunction or break down and have to be repaired. However, in most instances when the computer fails, it is due to human error and is not the fault of the computer at all.

[5] In the fourth place, **general-purpose computers** can be programmed to solve various types of problems because of their flexibility. One of the

Unit 4 Computer capabilities and limitations

most important reasons why computers are so widely used today is that almost every big problem can be solved by solving a number of little problems – one after another.

[6] Finally, a computer, unlike a human being, has no intuition. A person may suddenly find the answer to a problem without working out too many of the details, but a computer can only proceed as it has been programmed to.

[7] Using the very limited capabilities possessed by all computers, the task of producing a university payroll, for instance, can be done quite easily. The following kinds of things need be done for each employee on the payroll. First: Input information about the employee such as wage rate, hours worked, tax rate, unemployment insurance, and pension deductions. Second: Do some simple arithmetic and decision making operations. Third: Output a few printed lines on a cheque. By repeating this process over and over again, the payroll will eventually be completed.

Exercises

1 Main idea

Which statement best expresses the main idea of the text? Why did you eliminate the other choices?

☐ 1. The most elaborate of computers must be programmed in order to be useful.

☐ 2. It is important to know what a computer can and cannot do.

☐ 3. A computer is useless without a programmer to tell it what to do.

2 Understanding the passage

Decide whether the following statements are true or false (T/F) by referring to the information in the text. Then make the necessary changes so that the false statements become true.

T F
☐ ☐ 1. A computer cannot do anything until it has been programmed.

☐ ☐ 2. A computer is a useless machine if its capabilities and limitations are unknown.

☐ ☐ 3. A computer can repeat the same operation over and over again forever if permitted.

	T	F	
4.	☐	☐	The speed at which different computer components function is considered to be one of the limitations of a computer.
5.	☐	☐	Computers do not usually make mistakes unless they break down.
6.	☐	☐	A computer can think and solve problems by itself.
7.	☐	☐	A computer is a single-purpose machine in that it cannot be programmed to solve various types of problems.
8.	☐	☐	Computers can solve big problems by following a series of simple steps.
9.	☐	☐	A computer usually solves problems by doing some mathematical and decision-making operations.
10.	☐	☐	Computers are used because they are fast and exact.

3 Locating information

Find the passages in the text where the following ideas are expressed. Give the line references.

.... 1. A computer can do the same operation millions of times without stopping.
.... 2. A computer must work out the details of a problem before reaching a solution.
.... 3. A computer needs to be told what to do.
.... 4. Computers can solve all kinds of different problems.
.... 5. Knowledge of a computer's capabilities and limitations is important.
.... 6. A computer can process information very rapidly.
.... 7. Computers are exact and dependable.
.... 8. Input and output devices operate more slowly than the arithmetic and decision-making devices.

4 Contextual reference

Look back at the text and find out what the words in **bold** typeface refer to.

1. no matter how capable **it** is   (l. 5)   ....
2. to **those** for arithmetic operations   (l. 14) ....
3. **they** are man-made machines   (l. 23) ....
4. **they** sometimes malfunction   (l. 24) ....
5. because of **their** flexibility   (l. 28) ....

Unit 4 Computer capabilities and limitations

6. **one** after another (l. 31) ....
7. one after **another** (l. 31) ....
8. as **it** has been programmed to (l. 34) ....
9. **The following kinds of things**
   need be done (l. 38) ....
10. By repeating **this process** (l. 43) ....

5 Understanding words

Refer back to the text and find synonyms (i.e. words with a similar meaning) for the following words.

1. job (l. 2) ....
2. comprehended (l. 7) ....
3. clever (l. 13) ....
4. cases (l. 25) ....
5. salary sheet (l. 39) ....

Now refer back to the text and find antonyms (i.e. words with an opposite meaning) for the following words.

6. basic (l. 5) ....
7. exceptional (l. 16) ....
8. run well (l. 24) ....
9. slowly (l. 33) ....
10. employer (l. 39) ....

6 Word forms

First choose the appropriate form of the words to complete the sentences. Then check the differences of meaning in your dictionary.

1. repetition, repeat, repetitive, repeatedly, repeating
   a. There are some people who .... arrive late to class whenever they're working on a program because they forget the time.
   b. A computer can do .... operations without getting tired or bored.
   c. ...., which can be a boring and unproductive task has been eliminated with the use of computers.
   d. A computer can .... the same operation over and over again accurately without becoming bored or tired.

2. comparison, compare, comparable, comparatively, comparative
   a. Renting a computer isn't .... to owning one.
   b. Computers can .... numbers.

c. There is sometimes very little .... to be made between two different brand-name microcomputers.

d. The difference in price of microcomputers from different manufacturers can be .... small.

3. repairs, repaired, repairable, repair
   a. When the computer is down it needs to be ....
   b. Electronic equipment often takes a long time to ....
   c. .... to a computer system are often done by the same company who manufactured the system.

4. accuracy, accurate, accurately
   a. A computer is always .... in its results if well prepared.
   b. .... is one of the advantages of using computers in research or in statistical analysis.
   c. Computers can produce results quickly and ....

7a Content review

Match the words in column A with the appropriate statement in column B.

A	B
☐ 1. decision-making operations	a. can solve different types of problems
☐ 2. programmer	b. all the equipment needed input, process and output information
☐ 3. general-purpose computers	
☐ 4. computer system	c. those which compare numbers
	d. decides what the program is to be.

7b Content review

Decide which of the following statements are computer capabilities or limitations. (C or L in each box.)

☐ 1. directed and controlled
☐ 2. must be told what to do
☐ 3. capable of doing repetitive operations
☐ 4. never gets bored or tired

- [ ] 5. fast and careful
- [ ] 6. input-output operations are slower
- [ ] 7. very accurate and dependable
- [ ] 8. man-made machine
- [ ] 9. can solve different types of problems
- [ ] 10. finds a solution after working out all the details
- [ ] 11. can't think for itself
- [ ] 12. producing a payroll is an easy task

8 Focus review

Focus C   Organizing information
On a separate sheet, organize the information in Unit 4, 'Computer Capabilities and Limitations', under *main idea(s)*, *major details* and *minor details*.

UNIT 5

Hardware and software

[1] In order to use computers effectively to solve problems in our environment, **computer systems** are devised. A 'system' implies a good mixture of integrated parts working together to form a useful whole. Computer systems may be discussed in two parts.

[2] The first part is **hardware** – the physical, electronic, and electromechanical devices that are thought of and recognized as 'computers'. The second part is **software** – the programs that control and coordinate the activities of the computer hardware and that direct the processing of data.

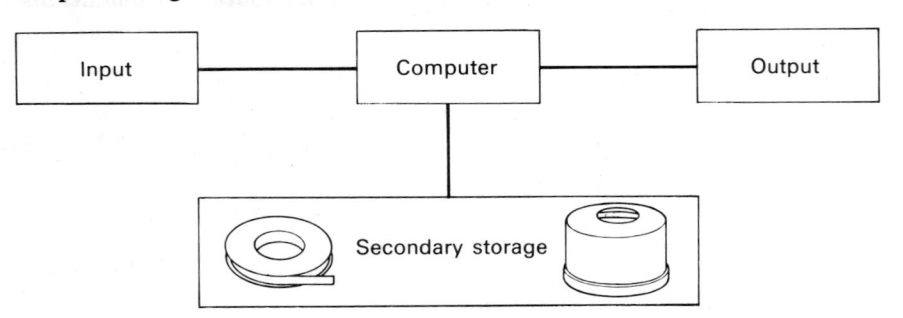

```
┌─────────┐      ┌──────────┐      ┌─────────┐
│  Input  │──────│ Computer │──────│ Output  │
└─────────┘      └──────────┘      └─────────┘
                       │
            ┌──────────┴──────────┐
            │  Secondary storage  │
            └─────────────────────┘
```

Figure 5.1 Hardware components of a basic computer system

[3] Figure 5.1 shows diagrammatically the basic components of computer hardware joined together in a computer system. The centerpiece is called either the computer, the **processor**, or usually the **central processing unit** (**CPU**). The term 'computer' usually refers to those parts of the hardware in which calculations and other data manipulations are performed, and to the internal memory in which data and instructions are stored during the actual execution of programs. The various **peripherals**, which include **input** and/or **output** devices, various **secondary memory** devices, and so on, are attached to the CPU.

[4] Computer software can be divided into two very broad categories – **systems software** and **applications software**. The former is often simply referred to as 'systems'. These, when brought into internal memory, direct the computer to perform tasks. The latter may be provided along with the hardware by a systems supplier as part of a

computer product designed to answer a specific need in certain areas. These complete hardware/software products are called **turnkey systems**.

[5] The success or failure of any computer system depends on the skill with which the hardware and software components are selected and blended. A poorly chosen system can be a monstrosity incapable of performing the tasks for which it was originally acquired.

Exercises

1 Main idea
Which statement best expresses the main idea of the text? Why did you eliminate the other choices?

☐ 1. Only hardware is necessary to make up a computer system.

☐ 2. Software alone doesn't constitute a computer system.

☐ 3. A computer system needs both hardware and software to be complete.

2 Understanding the passage
Indicate whether the following ideas are stated or not stated (S/NS) in the text.

S NS
☐ ☐ 1. A system implies a good mixture of parts working together.

☐ ☐ 2. Input and output devices operate more slowly than the decision-making devices.

☐ ☐ 3. The control unit and the arithmetic-logical unit are part of the processor.

☐ ☐ 4. The 'computer' is the hardware.

☐ ☐ 5. Software is the programs on cards, tapes and disks.

☐ ☐ 6. The processor is usually referred to as the CPU.

☐ ☐ 7. The word 'computer' means the processor and the internal memory.

☐ ☐ 8. Systems software is usually referred to as programs.

☐ ☐ 9. Complete hardware/software products are called turnkey systems.

☐ ☐ 10. Computers process specially prepared items of information.

3 Locating information

Find the passages in the text where the following ideas are expressed. Give the line references.

.... 1. The hardware consists of the physical devices of the computer.
.... 2. In order to solve problems, an appropriate computer system must be developed.
.... 3. The 'computer' is the CPU and the internal memory.
.... 4. The success or failure of a computer system depends on the proper mixture of hardware and software.
.... 5. There are two parts to a computer system.
.... 6. Computer software can be divided into two parts.
.... 7. The software is the programs.
.... 8. The peripheral devices are attached to the CPU.

4 Contextual reference

Look back at the text and find out what the words in **bold** typeface refer to.

1. Computer systems may be discussed **in two parts** *(l. 4)* ....
2. **that** are thought of *(l. 6)* ....
3. **that** control and coordinate *(l. 7)* ....
4. and **that** direct the processing *(l. 8)* ....
5. **in which** calculations *(l. 14)* ....
6. **in which** data and instructions *(l. 15)* ....
7. **The former** is often simply referred to *(l. 20)* ....
8. **These**, when brought into *(l. 21)* ....
9. **The latter** may be provided along with *(l. 22)* ....
10. for which **it** was originally acquired *(l. 29)* ....

5 Understanding words

Refer back to the text and find synonyms for the following words.

1. developed *(l. 2)* ....
2. infers *(l. 2)* ....
3. joined *(l. 3)* ....
4. chosen *(l. 27)* ....

Now refer back to the text and find antonyms for the following words.

5. segregated *(l. 3)* ....
6. useless *(l. 3)* ....
7. narrow *(l. 19)* ....
8. well *(l. 28)* ....

6 Word forms

First choose the appropriate form of the words to complete the sentences. Then check the differences of meaning in your dictionary.

1. integration, integrate, integrated, integrating
   a. Some computer manufacturers have .... both input and output devices into one terminal.
   b. The success of any computer system depends on the .... of all its parts to form a useful whole.
   c. .... input and output devices into one peripheral has reduced the area needed for a computer installation.

2. coordination, coordinate, coordinated, coordinating, coordinator
   a. The control unit of a processor .... the flow of information between the arithmetic unit and the memory.
   b. .... the many activities in a computer department is the job of the department head.
   c. The .... of a language institute has assistants to help him and may have access to a computer to help him with the .... of the many programs, timetables, space and student results.

3. diagram, diagrammatic, diagrammatically, diagrammed
   a. Very often manufacturers provide .... representations of the internal workings of a computer.
   b. A .... is a drawing that shows how something is arranged rather than what it actually looks like.
   c. A few ideas have been .... for you in this book.

4. interchange, interchangeable, interchangeably, interchanged.
   a. The words 'arithmetic-logic' and 'arithmetic-logical' can be used ....
   b. There is often an .... of ideas among computer scientists.
   c. There is a big difference between an input and an output. These cannot be ....

5. division, divide, divisible
   a. It is often difficult for computer science students to .... their time up proportionally between studying and programming.
   b. Are all numbers .... by three?
   c. There is always a .... of labour within a computer company.

7a Content review
Match the words in column A with the words or statements in column B.

A	B
☐ 1. hardware	a. the computer
☐ 2. software	b. input/output and secondary memory devices
☐ 3. processor	c. short for central processing unit
☐ 4. peripherals	d. physical electronic and electromagnetic devices
☐ 5. systems software	
☐ 6. applications software	e. hardware plus software
☐ 7. turnkey systems	f. hardware/software packages
☐ 8. computer systems	g. used for a specific job
☐ 9. CPU	h. direct the computer
	i. the programs

7b Content review
Use the following diagram which shows the relationship between the system and its parts to complete the paragraph.

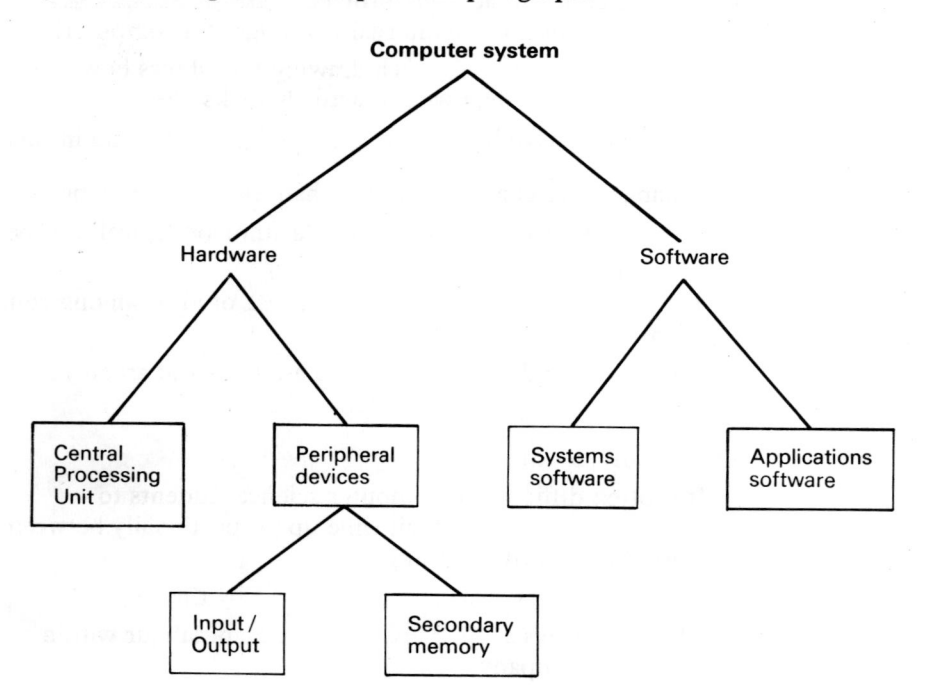

```
                    Computer system
                   /               \
              Hardware           Software
              /     \            /        \
    Central    Peripheral    Systems    Applications
    Processing  devices      software   software
    Unit         /    \
            Input/   Secondary
            Output   memory
```

A computer system consists of two components: ....
and .... Each component is subdivided into different
parts. The Central Processing Unit and the ....
constitute the .... component. Systems software and
.... comprise the .... component.
Devices that are used for secondary storage are considered part of the
.... component. These devices along with Input and
Output devices are referred to as .... devices.

8 Focus review

Focus C   Organizing information

On a separate sheet, organize the information in Unit 5, 'Hardware and Software', under *main idea(s)*, *major details* and *minor details*.

FOCUS D

Word formation – Prefixes

We have already seen how suffixes change the part of speech of a word. Let us now consider some *prefixes*, their usual meanings, and how they change the meanings of English words.

PREFIXES				
NEGATIVE AND POSITIVE	**SIZE**	**LOCATION**	**TIME AND ORDER**	**NUMBER**
un-	semi-	inter-	pre-	mono-
non-	mini-	super-	ante-	bi-
in-	micro-	trans-	fore-	hex-
dis-		ex-	post-	oct-
re-		extra-		multi-
		mid-		

Exercise 1

Study these tables and try to find additional examples. Use your dictionary if necessary.

	Negative and positive prefixes		
	PREFIX	MEANING	EXAMPLES
Negative	un- in- im- il- ir-	not, not good enough	unmagnetized, unpunched incomplete impossible illegal irregular, irrelevant
	non-	not connected with	non-programmable, non-impact
	mis-	bad, wrong	mispronounce
	dis-	opposite feeling opposite action	disagree disconnect
	anti-	against	antisocial
	de-	reduce, reverse	demagnetize, decode
	under-	too little	underestimate
Positive	re- over-	do again too much	reorganize overheat

Focus D Word formation – Prefixes

Prefixes of size

PREFIX	MEANING	EXAMPLES
semi-	half, partly	semiconductor
equi-	equal	equidistant
maxi-	big	maxicomputer
micro-	small	microcomputer
mini-	little	minicomputer
macro-	large	macroeconomics
mega-	large	megabyte

Prefixes of location

PREFIX	MEANING	EXAMPLES
inter-	between, among	interface, interactive
super-	over	supersonic
trans-	across	transmit, transfer
ex-	out	exclude, extrinsic
extra-	beyond	extraordinary
sub-	under	subschema
infra-	below	infra-red
peri-	around	peripheral

Prefixes of time and order

PREFIX	MEANING	EXAMPLES
ante-	before	antecedent
pre-	before	prefix
prime-	first	primary, primitive
post-	after	postdated
retro-	backward	retroactive

Prefixes of numbers

PREFIX	MEANING	EXAMPLES
semi-	half	semicircle
mono-	one	monochromatic
bi-	two	binary
tri-	three	triangle
quad-	four	quadruple
penta-	five	Pentagon
hex-	six	hexadecimal
septem-	seven	September
oct-	eight	octal
dec-	ten	decimal
multi-	many	multiprogramming, multiplexor

Other prefixes

PREFIX	MEANING	EXAMPLES
pro-	for	program
auto-	self	automatic
co-	together	coordinate
neo-	new	neoclassical
pan-	all	Pan-American

Exercise 2
Read the following sentences and underline all the prefixes. Then try to find out what the prefixes mean by referring back to the tables you have just completed.

1. Non-impact printers are inexpensive and silent.
2. Tape-marks are unmagnetized reflective strips stuck onto the tape.
3. The octal and the hexadecimal systems are number systems used as a form of shorthand in reading groups of four binary digits.
4. The internal storage locations of a computer are called its primary memory.
5. Multiprogramming is when more than one program can be present at different storage locations of the memory at the same time.
6. Peripheral devices can be either input devices (such as card readers) or output devices (such as printers).
7. The decoder (a component of the control unit) takes the coded instruction and breaks it down into the individual commands necessary to carry it out.
8. Microcomputers are becoming very important in small business applications.
9. A tape drive transmits the electromagnetic impulses to the memory of the computer.
10. Semiconductor materials are used in the making of transistors.

Exercise 3
Fill in the blanks with the correct prefix from the following list. Use the glossary at the end of the book to help you.

multi-	deci-	sub-	inter-
semi-	mono-	mega-	auto-
mini-	de-	inter-	prim-

Focus D Word formation – Prefixes

1. ....byte means one million bytes.
2. ....plexing is when many electrical signals are combined and carried on only one optical link.
3. Blocks are separated from each other by marks called ....block gaps.
4. The number system we use in everyday life is the ....mal system which has a base of 10.
5. CRT terminals are very useful ....active devices for use in airline reservations.
6. Some screens are ....chromatic whereas others produce multicolour pictorial graphics.
7. The complete description of the logical structure of data is called the schema and the description of the parts, the ....schema.
8. The main storage locations of a computer are called its ....ary storage.
9. The small ferrite rings called cores have two states: they can be either magnetized or ....magnetized.
10. The introduction of chips or ....conductor memories made it possible to reduce the size of the computer.

Exercise 4

Read the following paragraph and as you read it, complete the table on page 62 and underline the prefixes.

Computers may have a short history but prior to their development, there were many other ways of doing calculations. These calculations were done using devices that are still used today; the slide rule being a perfect example, not to mention the ten fingers of the hands. These machines, unlike computers, are non-electronic and were replaced by faster calculating devices. It wasn't until the mid-1940s that the first digital computer was built. The post-war industrial boom saw the development of computers take shape. By the 1960s, computers were faster than their predecessors and semiconductors had replaced vacuum tubes only to be replaced in a few years by tiny integrated circuit boards. Due to microminiaturization in the 1970s, these circuits were etched onto wafer-thin rectangular pieces of silicon. This integrated circuitry is known as a chip and is used in microcomputers of all kinds. It has been forecasted, by the end of this decade, exceptionally faster and smaller computers will replace those in use today.

Focus D Word formation – Prefixes

Prefixes				
NEGATIVE AND POSITIVE	SIZE	LOCATION	TIME AND ORDER	NUMBER
unlike			*post-war*	

Exercise 5 Review of suffixes

Read the following paragraph and as you read it, complete the table below and underline the suffixes.

A computer can solve a series of problems and make hundreds, even thousands, of logical decisions without becoming tired or bored. It can find the solution to a problem in a fraction of the time it takes a human being to do the job. A computer can replace people in dull, routine tasks, but it has no originality; it works according to the instructions given to it and cannot exercise any value judgments. There are times when a computer seems to operate like a mechanical 'brain', but its achievements are limited by the minds of human beings. A computer cannot do anything unless a person tells it what to do and gives it the appropriate information; but because electric pulses can move at the speed of light, a computer can carry out vast numbers of arithmetic-logical operations almost instantaneously. A person can do everything a computer can do, but in many cases that person would be dead long before the job was finished.

Suffixes			
NOUNS	VERBS	ADJECTIVES	ADVERBS
computer *information*		*electronic*	

SECTION 3

Kinds of computers

UNIT 6

Mainframes

[1] Large computer systems, or **mainframes,** as they are referred to in the field of computer science, are those computer systems found in **computer installations** processing immense amounts of data. These powerful computers make use of very high-speed main memories into which data and programs to be dealt with are transferred for rapid access. These powerful machines have a larger repertoire of more complex instructions which can be executed more quickly. Whereas smaller computers may take several steps to perform a particular operation, a larger machine may accomplish the same thing with one instruction.

[2] These computers can be of two types: **digital** or **analog**. The digital computer or general-purpose computer as it is often known, makes up about 90 per cent of the large computers now in use. It gets its name because the data that are presented to it are made up of a code consisting of **digits** – single-character numbers. The digital computer is like a gigantic cash register in that it can do calculations in steps, one after another at tremendous speed and with great accuracy. Digital computer **programming** is by far the most commonly used in electronic **data processing** for business or statistical purposes. The analog computer works something like a car speedometer, in that it continuously works out calculations. It is used essentially for problems involving measurements. It can simulate, or imitate different measurements by electronic means. Both of these computer types – the digital and the analog – are made up of electronic components that may require a large room to accommodate them. At present, the digital computer is capable of doing anything the analog once did. Moreover, it is easier to program and cheaper to operate. A new type of scientific computer system called the **hybrid computer** has now been produced that combines the two types into one.

[3] Really powerful computers continue to be bulky and require special provision for their housing, refrigeration systems, air filtration and power supplies. This is because much more space is taken up by the input/output devices – the magnetic tape and disk units and other peripheral equipment – than by the electronic components that do not

make up the bulk of the machine in a powerful installation. The power consumption of these machines is also quite high, not to mention the price that runs into hundreds of thousands of dollars. The future will bring great developments in the mechanical devices associated with computer systems. For a long time these have been the weak link, from the point of view of both efficiency and reliability.

Exercises

1 Main idea

Which statement best expresses the main idea of the text? Why did you eliminate the other choices?

☐ 1. Hybrid computers are a combination of digital and analog computers.

☐ 2. Digital computers are used more than any other type of computer.

☐ 3. There are three types of mainframes.

☐ 4. Analog computers can do more varied work than digital or hybrid computers.

2 Understanding the passage

Decide whether the following sentences are true or false (T/F) by referring to the information in the text. Then make the necessary changes so that the false statements become true.

T   F

☐ ☐ 1. A mainframe is the type of computer that can sit on top of a desk.

☐ ☐ 2. Mainframes are very powerful and can execute jobs very rapidly and easily.

☐ ☐ 3. Digital computers are used more than analog computers.

☐ ☐ 4. The analog computer is far smaller than a digital computer and therefore occupies very little space.

☐ ☐ 5. The hybrid computer is a combination of both the digital and the analog computer.

☐ ☐ 6. The analog computer does its calculations one step at a time.

Unit 6 Mainframes

T	F	
☐	☐	7. The digital computer continuously works out calculations.
☐	☐	8. Mainframes are huge powerful machines whose peripheral equipment takes up a lot of space.
☐	☐	9. Mainframes are expensive to buy and to operate.
☐	☐	10. Mainframe technology has reached the end of the road. No further development is needed.

3 Locating information

Find the passages in the text where the following ideas are expressed. Give the line references.

.... 1. Smaller computers may take longer to perform an operation.
.... 2. More technological development is necessary in the mechanical devices associated with computer systems.
.... 3. Mainframes can operate quickly and execute more complex instructions.
.... 4. The hybrid computer is a combination of both digital and analog computers.
.... 5. Digital computers are used more than analog computers.
.... 6. Mainframes are large powerful computers.
.... 7. An analog computer is comparable to a car speedometer in the way it operates.
.... 8. Digital computers do calculations, one after another, quickly and exactly.

4 Contextual reference

Look back at the text and find out what the words in **bold** typeface refer to.

1. **which** can be executed (l. 7) ....
2. as **it** is often known (l. 12) ....
3. **that** are presented to it (l. 14) ....
4. in that **it** can do calculations (l. 16) ....
5. in that **it** continuously works out (l. 20) ....
6. **Both** of these computer types (l. 23) ....
7. **that** may require a large room (l. 24) ....
8. **that** combines the two types (l. 29) ....
9. require special provision for **their** housing (l. 31) ....
10. **that** runs into thousands of dollars (l. 37) ....

5 Understanding words
Refer back to the text and find synonyms for the following words.

1. area   (l. 2)   ....
2. acted on   (l. 7)   ....
3. do   (l. 9)   ....
4. composed of   (l. 15) ....
5. principally   (l. 21) ....

Now refer back to the text and find antonyms for the following words.

6. ignored   (l. 5)   ....
7. seldom   (l. 12) ....
8. little   (l. 16) ....
9. small   (l. 30) ....
10. weak   (l. 35) ....

6 Word forms
First choose the appropriate form of the words to complete the sentences. Then check the differences of meaning in your dictionary.

1. permission, permit, permissible, permitted
   a. It is usually not .... to smoke in a computer installation.
   b. Computers .... people to use their time more effectively.
   c. Building .... is usually required before starting any renovations to a building for a computer department.

2. continuation, continue, continuing, continuously
   a. If microcomputer sales .... to increase, it won't be long before every household has one.
   b. Computers can do repetitive operations .... without getting bored.
   c. There is a .... interest in discovering new areas where computers can be used.

3. measurement, measure, measured, measurable
   a. The analog computer is essentially used for problems involving ....
   b. Because computer equipment is often bulky, the area used for a computer installation must be .... out carefully.
   c. The number of employees a computer company has can be seen as a .... of its success in the business world.

4. association, associate, associated
   a. Computers are .... with speed and accuracy.
   b. There are many computer .... around the world to which computer professionals belong.
   c. Business .... in different cities often communicate with each other via their computers.

5. efficiency, efficient, efficiently
   a. Using a hand calculator to do simple mathematics is an .... way of working.
   b. Computers can solve problems faster and more .... than humans.
   c. .... is important in any service industry.

7 Content review

Try to think of a definition for each of these items before checking them in the Glossary. Then complete the following statements with the appropriate words. (Some can be used more than once.) Make sure you use the correct form, i.e. singular or plural.

mainframe	computer installation	digits
hybrid computer	code	programming
digital	analog	

1. The .... system is a computer which has combined the features of both the .... and .... computer. It is used mainly in scientific research.

2. .... computers get their name from the word .... These are single character numbers that make up the .... in which the data are presented to the computer for processing.

3. .... are usually found in large ....

4. The most commonly used language of .... in the business community is ....

8 Focus review

Focus C   Organizing information

On a separate sheet, organize the information in Unit 6, 'Mainframes', under *main idea(s), major details* and *minor details*.

FOCUS E

Listing

It is important when reading to recognize and understand the relationship in which sentences and groups of sentences combine to present information. This information may be linked by means of a *connective word* or *marker*.

Making a list, enumerating, and giving instructions, indicates a cataloguing of what is being said. It is important to note that most enumerations belong to clearly defined sets. The following table is a list of the markers that can be used to show the order in which things are to be said.

LISTING MARKERS
1, 2, 3, etc. one, two, three, etc. first(ly), second(ly), third(ly)
in the first/second/third place
another, next, then furthermore, afterwards, moreover
lastly/finally to begin/start with, and to conclude
first and foremost　　　　} mark the beginning first and most important(ly) } of a descending order
above all　　　　　} mark the end of last but not least } an ascending order

There are many ways of showing sequential relationships. Those given in the table above are not the only ones, they are the most common ones used in listing or enumerating. The **-ly** forms are usually used when listing.

Sample paragraph

More and more police departments are now using sophisticated devices to help control the increasing crime rate. Some of these devices are: **firstly**, a computer terminal inside a police vehicle to answer an officer's questions; **secondly**, a computer-controlled display unit for displaying fingerprints; and **thirdly**, educational systems for police officers such as terminals, enabling them to verify changes in laws, rules and regulations.

The computer memory of many law enforcement systems contain all kinds of information. **First and foremost**, it has data on stolen items such as cars, license plates and property. **Second**, it has information on missing persons and wanted fugitives. **Last but not least**, it contains information on political extremist groups and their activities.

It goes without saying that computers have certainly revolutionized police work by providing access to millions of items of information with the least possible delay and speeding up the process of apprehending suspicious-looking characters.

Exercise 1

The following paragraph is an excerpt from paragraph 3 of Unit 1 'What Is a Computer?' While reading this paragraph underline the listing markers.

Computers are thought to have many remarkable powers. However, most computers, whether large or small have three basic capabilities. First, computers have circuits for performing arithmetic operations, such as addition, subtraction, division, multiplication and exponentiation. Second, computers have a means of communicating with the user. After all, if we couldn't feed information in and get results back, those machines wouldn't be of much use. Third, computers have circuits which can make decisions. The computer can only decide three things: 1. Is one number less than another?   2. Are two numbers equal?   and 3. Is one number greater than another?

Exercise 2

Complete the following table by referring back to paragraphs 2, 3, 4, 5, 6 of the text on 'Computer Capabilities and Limitations' (Unit 4).

LISTING MARKER	CHARACTERISTICS
1.	can do repetitive operations
2. Secondly	
3.	can calculate answers accurately
4.	can be programmed to solve various problems
5. Finally	

Exercise 3

Complete the following paragraph by filling in the blanks with appropriate listing markers.

Computers can do wonders, but they can waste a lot of money unless careful consideration goes into buying them. Any businessman thinking of buying a computer system should .... admit he knows very little about computers. ...., he must realize that the computer salesman doesn't know how his business works. ...., that he should get outside advice is a must, not necessarily from consultants but from other executives who have had recent experience in buying a computer system. .... he should try to see systems similar to ones under consideration in operation. Because his operations will have differences that must be accommodated, he should .... find out what would be involved in upgrading a system. .... important thing to know before buying a computer is the financial situation of the supplier because computer companies come and go and not all are financially stable. ...., the prospective buyer should demand that every detail be covered in writing, including hardware and software if they are supplied by different companies. There's nothing wrong with computers, it's how and why they are used that can cause problems.

UNIT 7

Minicomputers

[1] Until the mid-1960s, digital computers were powerful, physically large and expensive. What was really needed though, were computers of less power, a smaller memory capacity and without such a large array of peripheral equipment. This need was partially satisfied by the rapid improvement in performance of the semi-conductor devices (transistors), and their incredible reduction in size, cost and power; all of which led to the development of the **minicomputer** or **mini** for short. Although there is no exact definition of a minicomputer, it is generally understood to refer to a computer whose mainframe is physically small, has a fixed word length between 8 and 32 **bits** and costs less than U.S. $100,000 for the central processor. The amount of **primary storage** available optionally in minicomputer systems ranges from 32-512K* bytes; however, some systems allow this memory to be expanded even further.

[2] A large number of peripherals have been developed especially for use in systems built around minicomputers; they are sometimes referred to as **miniperipherals**. These include **magnetic tape cartridges** and **cassettes**, small disk units and a large variety of printers and **consoles**.

[3] Many minicomputers are used merely for a fixed application and run only a single program. This is changed only when necessary either to correct errors or when a change in the design of the system is introduced. Since the operating environment for most minis is far less varied and complex than large mainframes, it goes without saying that the software and peripheral requirements differ greatly from those of a computer which runs several hundred ever-changing jobs a day. The operating systems of minis also usually provide system access to either a single user or to a limited number of users at a time.

[4] Since many minis are employed in **real-time processing**, they are usually provided with operating systems that are specialized for this purpose. For example, most minis have an **interrupt feature** which allows a program to be interrupted when they receive a special signal indicating that any one of a number of external events, to which they are preprogrammed to respond, has occurred. When the interrupt occurs, the computer stores enough information about the job in process

Unit 7 Minicomputers

to resume operation after it has responded to the interruption. Because minicomputer systems have been used so often in **real-time applications**, other aspects of their design have changed; that is, they usually possess the hardware capability to be connected directly to a large variety of measurement instruments, to analog and digital converters, to **microprocessors**, and ultimately, to an even larger mainframe in order to analyse the collected data.

* 1K is defined as $2^{10} = 1024$; thus $32K = 32 \times 2^{10} = 2^5 \times 2^{10} = 2^{15} = 32,768$.

Exercises

1 Main idea
Which statement best expresses the main idea of the text? Why did you eliminate the other choices?

☐ 1. Minicomputers are not as effective as mainframes.

☐ 2. Minicomputers are as useful as mainframes.

☐ 3. Minicomputers are not as big and expensive as mainframes.

☐ 4. Minicomputers will not be of any use in the future.

2 Understanding the passage
Indicate whether the following ideas are stated or not stated (S/NS) in the text.

S NS
☐ ☐ 1. The rapid development of transistors led to the development of minicomputers.

☐ ☐ 2. A minicomputer is said to be very much the same as a mainframe.

☐ ☐ 3. Special peripheral devices have been developed to go with minicomputers.

☐ ☐ 4. Minicomputers can understand more than one computer language.

☐ ☐ 5. Mainframe operating systems usually provide access to a number of users at the same time.

☐ ☐ 6. Minicomputers have specialized features because of the operations they execute.

74 Unit 7 Minicomputers

S   NS

☐   ☐   7. Minicomputers can be connected directly to various types of devices.

☐   ☐   8. Microcomputers were developed after mainframes.

☐   ☐   9. Minicomputers will be more popular in the future than mainframes.

☐   ☐   10. Operating minicomputers costs less than operating mainframes.

3 Locating information

Find the passages in the text where the following ideas are expressed. Give the line references.

.... 1. Various peripherals were developed to go with minicomputers.
.... 2. Minicomputers were developed after the mid-1960s.
.... 3. Minicomputers have specially built-in features that enable them to store information while responding to another operation.
.... 4. The improved performance of transistors led to the development of minicomputers.
.... 5. Minicomputers can be hooked up to larger mainframes if need be.
.... 6. Minicomputers are usually used for single-purpose jobs.
.... 7. Minicomputers are similar to mainframes except that they are smaller.
.... 8. Fewer people can use minicomputers at one time than mainframes.

4 Contextual reference

Look back at the text and find out what the words in **bold** typeface refer to.

1. **This need** was partially satisfied (l. 4) ....
2. **their** incredible reduction in size (l. 6) ....
3. **they** are sometimes referred to (l. 16) ....
4. **This** is changed only when necessary (l. 20) ....
5. differ greatly from **those** of a computer (l. 24) ....
6. **they** are usually provided with (l. 28) ....
7. when **they** receive a special signal (l. 31) ....
8. **to which** they are preprogrammed (l. 32) ....
9. other aspects of **their** design (l. 37) ....
10. **they** usually possess the hardware (l. 37) ....

Unit 7 Minicomputers

5 Understanding words

Refer back to the text and find synonyms for the following words.

1. range   (l. 3)   ....
2. unbelievable (l. 6)   ....
3. purpose   (l. 19)   ....
4. continue   (l. 35)   ....
5. forms   (l. 37)   ....

Now refer back to the text and find antonyms for the following words.

6. reduced   (l. 13)   ....
7. non-specific (l. 19)   ....
8. unaltering   (l. 25)   ....
9. not used   (l. 28)   ....
10. not happened (l. 34)   ....

6 Word forms

First choose the appropriate form of the words to complete the sentences. Then check the differences of meaning in your dictionary.

1. power, powerful, powerfully, powerless, powered
   a. There are many ways of producing ....
   b. Battery .... calculators occupy less space than their predecessors.
   c. A computer is a very .... machine.
   d. Computers are rendered .... if there isn't an emergency supply system in case of power failure.

2. partiality, partial, partially, part
   a. Some people are .... to certain computer companies because of the success rate.
   b. Sometimes only a .... of the data is necessary to solve a problem.
   c. The need for smaller memory capacity was .... satisfied by the improved performance of transistors.

3. generality, generalize, general, generally
   a. .... purpose computers are larger than minicomputers.
   b. It is the .... consensus of opinion that computers have improved the quality of life.
   c. Minicomputers are .... cheaper than mainframes.
   d. It is often easier to .... than to talk about specifics.

4. specialize, special, specially, specialist, specialization, specialized
   a. Computer .... is a must for most large-scale companies today.
   b. Magnetic tape cartridges are .... peripheral devices used with minicomputers.
   c. A computer processes .... prepared items of information.

5. change, changeable, changeably, changing
   a. Computer personnel often have to take refresher courses in the .... field of computer science.
   b. Many .... have taken place in the computer industry in the last decade.
   c. Memory and primary storage can be used inter-..................................

7 Content review

Match the words in column A with the words or statements in column B.

A	B
☐ 1. minicomputer	a. processing unit of microcomputer
☐ 2. primary memory	b. specialized secondary memory devices
☐ 3. miniperipherals	
☐ 4. cartridges	c. where operator can manually operate the computer
☐ 5. console	d. internal storage
☐ 6. microprocessors	e. fixed word length of 8–32 bits
	f. attached to minicomputers

8 Focus review

Focus C   Organizing information

On a separate sheet, organize the information in Unit 7, 'Minicomputers', under *main idea(s)*, *major details* and *minor details*.

UNIT 8

Microcomputers

[1] The early 1970s saw the birth of the **microcomputer**, or **micro** for short. The central processor of the micro, called the **microprocessor**, is built as a single **semiconductor device**; that is, the thousands of individual circuit elements necessary to perform all the logical and arithmetic functions of a computer are manufactured as a single **chip**. A complete microcomputer system is composed of a microprocessor, a memory and peripheral equipment. The processor, memory and electronic controls for the peripheral equipment are usually put together on a single or on a few printed **circuit boards**. Systems using microprocessors can be hooked up together to do the work that until recently only minicomputer systems were capable of doing. Micros generally have somewhat simpler and less flexible instruction sets than minis, and are typically much slower. Different micros are available with 4-, 8-, 12-, 16-bit word lengths. Similarly, minis are available with word lengths up to 32 bits. Although minis can be equipped with much larger **primary memory** sizes, micros are becoming more powerful and converging with minicomputer technology.

[2] The extremely low price of micros has opened up entirely new areas of application for computers. Only 20 years or so ago, a central processing unit of medium capability sold for a few hundred thousand dollars (U.S.), and now some microprocessors sell for as cheaply as $10. Of course, by the time you have a usable microcomputer system, the price will be somewhere between $500 and $10,000 depending on the display unit, secondary storage, and whatever other peripherals are needed.

[3] The available range of microcomputer systems is evolving more rapidly than minicomputers. Because of their incredibly low price, it is now possible to use only a small fraction of the computer's capability in a particular system application and still be far ahead financially of any other way of getting the job done. For example, thousands of industrial robots are in use today, and the number is growing very rapidly as this relatively new industry improves the price and performance of its products by using the latest microcomputers.

[4] Even though the software available for most microcomputer systems is very limited – more so than for minis – it does not discourage their use in the many high-volume, fixed applications for which programming is

essentially a 'one shot deal' as is the case in the space shuttle program. In addition to their extensive use in control systems of all types, they are destined for many new uses from more complex calculators to automobile engine operation and medical diagnostics. They are already used in automobile emission control systems and are the basis of many TV game attachments. There is also a rapidly growing market for personal computers whose application potential in education is only just beginning to be exploited.

[5] It would seem that the limits for microcomputer applications have by no means been reached. There are those who predict that the home and hobby computer markets will grow into a multi-billion dollar enterprise within a decade or so. It would also appear that performance of microprocessors could well increase ten-fold before 1990 while prices for micros could decrease by as much.

Exercises

1 Main idea
Which statement best expresses the main idea of the text? Why did you eliminate the other choices?

☐ 1. Microcomputers will be everywhere in the future.

☐ 2. There is no limit to what microcomputers can do.

☐ 3. Microcomputers are cheap, reliable and efficient.

☐ 4. Microcomputers are far superior to minicomputers.

2 Understanding the passage
Indicate whether the following ideas are stated or not stated (S/NS) in the text.

S NS
☐ ☐   1. Microcomputers were developed after minicomputers.
☐ ☐   2. The processor of a microcomputer is printed on a chip.
☐ ☐   3. A mainframe uses more power than a microcomputer.
☐ ☐   4. Microcomputers can do the work done by minicomputers.
☐ ☐   5. Microcomputers have the same memory capacity as minicomputers and can be hooked up to a variety of peripherals.
☐ ☐   6. Microcomputers are cheaper than minicomputers.

Unit 8 Microcomputers

S	NS	
☐	☐	7. Many different types of industries are using microcomputers to do their work.
☐	☐	8. Microcomputers are now used in sophisticated toys and games.
☐	☐	9. Because of microminiaturization, mainframes now occupy less space.
☐	☐	10. By the end of this century microcomputers will be cheaper, better and probably used in every aspect of life.

3 Locating information
Find the passages in the text where the following ideas are expressed. Give the line references.

.... 1. Microcomputers can do work that until quite recently was done by minicomputers.
.... 2. Microcomputers are mainly used for single-purpose jobs.
.... 3. The integrated circuitry of a microcomputer has been reduced to a chip.
.... 4. Microcomputer technology will continue to improve.
.... 5. Microcomputers are smaller, simpler and less flexible than minicomputers.
.... 6. Microcomputers are a very recent development in computer technology.
.... 7. Microcomputer systems are increasing faster than minicomputers.
.... 8. In the future, microprocessors will be cheaper, and their capacity and performance will be greater.

4 Contextual reference
Look back at the text and find out what the words in **bold** typeface refer to.

1. **that** until recently (l. 10) ....
2. Because of **their** incredibly low price (l. 26) ....
3. performance of **its** products (l. 31) ....
4. **it** does not discourage their use (l. 34) ....
5. it does not discourage **their** use (l. 34) ....
6. **for which** programming is essentially (l. 35) ....
7. In addition to **their** extensive use (l. 37) ....
8. **they** are destined for many new uses (l. 37) ....
9. **whose** application potential (l. 42) ....
10. **who** predict that (l. 45) ....

5 Understanding words

Refer back to the text and find synonyms for the following words.

1. single   (l. 4)   ....
2. connected   (l. 10)   ....
3. moderate   (l. 20)   ....
4. scope   (l. 25)   ....
5. intended   (l. 38)   ....

Now refer back to the text and find antonyms for the following words.

6. death   (l. 1)   ....
7. in part   (l. 18)   ....
8. worsens   (l. 31)   ....
9. earliest   (l. 32)   ....
10. increase   (l. 49)   ....

6 Word forms

First choose the appropriate form of the words to complete the sentences. Then check the differences of meaning in your dictionary.

1. completion, complete, completely, completed
    a. When you've .... this book, you should have a basic knowledge of computers and how they operate.
    b. There are car manufacturing plants that are .... operated by robots.
    c. A .... microcomputer system has a microprocessor, a memory and peripheral equipment.

2. simple, simplify, simply, simplest, simpler
    a. Microcomputers are usually .... to operate.
    b. A microcomputer may be .... to operate than a minicomputer.
    c. Using a computer to control the payroll will .... matters for many companies.

3. flexibility, flexible, flexibly, flex
    a. Because of their .... microcomputers are becoming more popular than minicomputers.
    b. Minicomputers have a more .... set of instructions than microcomputers.

4. finance, financial, financially
   a. The .... implications of leasing a computer may be less than owning one.
   b. Companies often borrow huge sums of money to .... large-scale projects to computerize their business.
   c. .... speaking, a microcomputer is more affordable than a minicomputer.

5. education, educational, educationally, educated
   a. There are many .... institutes that teach computer programming.
   b. It is possible that by the year 2000, a well-.................................. person will have to have a good knowledge of computer science.
   c. There are many fields of .... today that use computers as teaching tools.

7a Content review

Try to think of a definition for each of these items before checking them in the Glossary. Then complete the following statements with the appropriate words. (Some can be used more than once.) Make sure you use the correct form, i.e. singular or plural.

microcomputer	semiconductor	chip
microprocessor	circuit board	primary memory
minicomputer	micro	memory

1. .... are often referred to as .... for short.
2. A .... system is composed of a ...., ... and peripheral equipment.
3. The .... of a microcomputer is usually built as a single .... device known as a ....
4. Microcomputers have small .... and cannot be hooked up to as many peripherals as ....
5. A few .... are normally used for the processor, memory and electronic controls of peripherals for microcomputers.

7b Content review

Summarize the texts on 'Mainframes', 'Minicomputers' and 'Microcomputers' (Units 6, 7 & 8), by completing the following table.

Kinds of Computers

	MAINFRAMES	MINICOMPUTERS	MICROCOMPUTERS
When developed			*developed in the 70s*
Usage			*used in fixed applications*
Memory speed and capacity		*most primary memory ranges from 32–512K bytes*	
Electrical power method			*consumes little electrical power*
Price	*extremely high prices*		
Size			*small portable size*
Complexity of instructions	*very complex instructions which can be executed quickly*		
Number of users			*single user-personal computer*
Type of processing	*allows batch as well as real-time processing*		

FOCUS F

Making comparisons

1 Formation

There are several ways of showing that similarities or differences exist between or amongst things. The regular comparative and superlative of descriptive words, whether these are adjectives or adverbs, is formed as follows:

1. by adding the ending **-er** and **-est** to words of *one syllable*

   Examples

	ABSOLUTE	COMPARATIVE	SUPERLATIVE
Adjectives	new old big	newer older bigger	newest oldest biggest
Adverbs	soon late	sooner later	soonest latest

2. by placing the words **more** and **most** in front of words with *three* or *more syllables*

   Examples

	ABSOLUTE	COMPARATIVE	SUPERLATIVE
Adjectives	interesting	more interesting	most interesting
	convenient	more convenient	most convenient
	beautiful	more beautiful	most beautiful
Adverbs	easily	more easily	most easily
	carefully	more carefully	most carefully

3. words with *two syllables* may be like 1 or 2 above in that they will add the ending **-er** and **-est** if they end in **-y** or **-ly, -ow, -le** and **-er**. Most of the remaining words take **more** and **most** in front of them.

Example

	ABSOLUTE	COMPARATIVE	SUPERLATIVE
-y	happy funny	happier funnier	happiest funniest
-ly	early friendly	earlier friendlier	earliest friendliest
-ow	shallow narrow	shallower narrower	shallowest narrowest
-le	able gentle	abler gentler	ablest gentlest
-er	clever	cleverer	cleverest

N.B. Two-syllable adverbs ending in **-ly** take **more** or **most**

Example

quickly	more quickly	most quickly
slowly	more slowly	most slowly
badly	more badly	most badly

Example

	ABSOLUTE	COMPARATIVE	SUPERLATIVE
Remaining descriptive two-syllable words	careful careless boring awful complex	more careful more careless more boring more awful more complex	most careful most careless most boring most awful most complex

4. Some common two-syllable adjectives can have either type of formation.

Example

ABSOLUTE	COMPARATIVE	SUPERLATIVE
common	commoner more common	commonest most common
handsome	handsomer more handsome	handsomest most handsome

Focus F Making comparisons

ABSOLUTE	COMPARATIVE	SUPERLATIVE
polite	politer more polite	politest most polite
quiet	quieter more quiet	quietest most quiet

5. There are a small number of adjectives and adverbs that form the comparative and superlative using a different stem. These irregular comparisons are as follows:

Example

	ABSOLUTE	COMPARATIVE	SUPERLATIVE
Adjectives	bad far good many	worse further/farther better more	worst furthest/farthest best most
Adverbs	badly far little much well	worse further/farther less more better	worst furthest/farthest least most best

2 Use in sentences

There are many reasons for using comparisons in discourse. They may be used to show: a. equivalence; b. non-equivalence; c. one item compared with others; and d. parallel increase.

Equivalence

The following words or constructions are used to show equivalence (i.e. the same).

as . . . as	are similar	each
as many . . . as	equal to	either
as much . . . as	is like	all
the same . . . as	similar/ly	both
similar to	equal/ly	alike
the same	compare to/with	

Examples
1. Third-generation computers can do a thousand times **as many** calculations **as** first-generation computers.
2. Microcomputers are **as** efficient **as** minicomputers.

3. The term processor is **the same as** central processing unit.
4. The digital computer **is like** a huge cash register.
5. An analog computer and a car speedometer **are similar** in that they continuously work out calculations.
6. A microcomputer can sometimes cost **as much as** a minicomputer.
7. **Both** minicomputers and microcomputers can have a memory of 32K bytes.
8. A digital computer can be **compared to** a large cash register.
9. **All** computers have the same basic characteristics.
10. The time it takes a computer to solve a problem can **equal** months of work for man.

Non-equivalence

The following words and/or constructions are used to show non-equivalence (i.e. not the same).

not as . . . as	greater than	unequal (ly)
word + er than	not as many . . . as	unlike
more . . . than	neither . . . nor . . . as	not the same as
fewer . . . than	not as much . . . as	not all
less . . . than	not equal to	

Examples
1. Learning a computer language is **not as** difficult **as** it seems.
2. A mainframe is **bigger** and **more** expensive **than** a microcomputer.
3. For **less than** $10,000, you could have a very good microcomputer.
4. Ten years ago, there were **fewer** computers in use **than** today.
5. **Neither** minicomputers **nor** microcomputers could be as complex as large mainframes.
6. **Unlike** minicomputers, microcomputers are not very flexible.
7. An analog computer is **not the same as** a digital computer.
8. **Not all** businesses have computerized their accounting departments.

The superlative

The following words and/or constructions are used to show one item compared with others (i.e. the superlative).

the word + est	the most . . .	the least . . .

Focus F Making comparisons

Examples
1. Computer technology is **the fastest** growing technology in the world today.
2. Digital computer programming is **the** one **most commonly** used in data processing for business.
3. BASIC is probably **the least difficult** computer language to learn.

Parallel increase

The following words and/or constructions are used to show parallel increase (i.e. two comparatives).

| the (word+er) the ... the more ... the (word+er) the ... the less ... |

Examples
1. **The bigger** the computer, **the more complex** the operations it can do.
2. **The smaller** the problem, **the less challenging** it is to the computer programmer.

Exercise 1

The following sentences are taken from Unit 4 'Computer Capabilities and Limitations'. Decide whether each sentence expresses equivalence, non-equivalence, or the superlative, then underline the words expressing the comparison.

equivalence
1. Speeds for performing decision-making operations are <u>comparable to</u> those for arithmetic operations.
....
2. Even the most sophisticated computer, no matter how good it is, must be told what to do.
....
3. A computer can perform similar operations thousands of times, without becoming bored, tired or even careless.
....
4. For example, modern computers can solve certain classes of arithmetic problems millions of times faster than a skilled mathematician.
....
5. One of the most important reasons why computers are used so widely today is that almost every big problem can be solved by solving a number of little problems.
....
6. Finally, a computer, unlike a human being, has no intuition.

Exercise 2

Read the text on 'Microcomputers' (Unit 8) again, and as you read complete the table below by writing the sentence or that part of the sentence that expresses a comparison.

PARA	EQUIVALENCE	NON-EQUIVALENCE	SUPERLATIVE
[1]	1. *is built as a single semi-conductor device*	1.	
	2.	2.	
	3.	3. *micros are becoming more powerful*	
[2]	1.		
[3]		1.	1.
[4]	1. *as is the case in the space shuttle program*	1.	
		2. *from more complex calculations to*	
[5]	1.		

PART 2

Computer components

A computer has four basic components: input, processor, memory and output. The processor has two parts: the control unit which directs and controls the signals and commands inside the processor, and the arithmetic-logical unit which does the five arithmetic operations and the three decision-making operations.

In a computer, internal memory or primary memory refers to the storage locations inside the computer whereas secondary memory refers to the storage embodied in the peripherals. There are three types of internal memory: core, as in the mainframes; semiconductor or chip, as in microcomputers; and bubble memory. Secondary memory, on the other hand, may be classified as either sequential (tape) or direct-access (disk).

The input devices, whether they are card readers, tape drives, disk drives or terminals, enter the information into the computer. After the processor has operated on it, the output devices display the results of the computations on a printer or a terminal, or store them on tape or disk.

PART 2

Computer components

SECTION 4

The processor

UNIT 9

The Central Processing Unit

CONTROL UNIT
ARITHMETIC-LOGICAL UNIT
MEMORY or MAIN STORAGE

[1] It is common practice in computer science for the words 'computer' and 'processor' to be used interchangeably. More precisely, 'computer' refers to the **central processing unit (CPU)** together with an **internal memory**. The internal memory or **main storage**, control and processing components make up the heart of the computer system. Manufacturers design the CPU to control and carry out basic instructions for their particular computer.

[2] The CPU coordinates all the activities of the various components of the computer. It determines which operations should be carried out and in what order. The CPU can also retrieve information from **memory** and can store the results of manipulations back into the **memory unit** for later reference.

[3] In digital computers the CPU can be divided into two functional units called the **control unit (CU)** and the **arithmetic-logical unit (ALU)**. These two units are made up of electronic circuits with millions of switches that can be in one of two states, either on or off.

[4] The function of the control unit within the central processor is to transmit coordinating control signals and commands. The control unit is that portion of the computer that directs the sequence or step-by-step operations of the system, selects instructions and data from memory, interprets the program instructions, and controls the flow between main storage and the arithmetic-logical unit.

[5] The arithmetic-logical unit, on the other hand, is that portion of the computer in which the actual arithmetic operations, namely, addition, subtraction, multiplication, division and exponentiation, called for in the instructions are performed. It also performs some kinds of logical operations such as comparing or selecting information. All the operations of the ALU are under the direction of the control unit.

[6] Programs and the data on which the control unit and the ALU operate, must be in internal memory in order to be processed. Thus, if located on secondary memory devices such as disks or tapes, programs and data are first loaded into internal memory.

[7] Main storage and the CPU are connected to a **console**, where manual control operations can be performed by an **operator**. The console is an important, but special purpose, piece of equipment. It is used mainly when the computer is being started up, or during maintenance and repair. Many mini and micro systems do not have a console.

Exercises

1 Main idea

Which statement best expresses the main idea of the text? Why did you eliminate the other choices?

☐ 1. Main storage is not a part of the processor.

☐ 2. The CPU is made up of the control unit, the arithmetic-logical unit and internal memory.

☐ 3. The CPU is composed of the arithmetic-logical unit and control unit only.

2 Understanding the passage

Decide whether the following statements are true or false (T/F) by referring to the information in the text. Then make the necessary changes so that the false statements become true.

T F
☐ ☐ 1. The central processing unit is made up of three components.
☐ ☐ 2. The CPU is responsible for all the activities taking place within a computer.
☐ ☐ 3. The processor itself has three components.
☐ ☐ 4. The control unit directs the flow of information within the processor.
☐ ☐ 5. The arithmetic-logical unit of the processor is responsible for the interpretation of program instructions.
☐ ☐ 6. The arithmetic-logical unit is also responsible for choosing and comparing the appropriate information within a program.

T   F

☐ ☐   7. The processor cannot operate on any information if that information is not in main storage.

☐ ☐   8. Secondary memory and internal memory are located in the same place in the computer system.

☐ ☐   9. Only after the data has been processed by the CPU can results be transmitted to an output device.

☐ ☐ 10. Computers can solve problems more quickly if they operate on new information.

3 Locating information

Find the passages in the text where the following ideas are expressed. Give the line references.

.... 1. The processor is the control unit and the arithmetic-logical unit.
.... 2. The processor operates on information that is in internal storage.
.... 3. The CPU directs all the activities of the computer.
.... 4. The control unit coordinates the sequencing of events within the processor.
.... 5. The word 'computer' usually refers to the CPU plus internal memory.
.... 6. The CPU can get information from memory and put old or new information back into memory.
.... 7. The arithmetic-logical unit does the calculations and decision-making operations.

4 Contextual reference

Look back at the text and find out what the words in **bold** typeface refer to.

1. for **their** particular computer   (l. 6) ....
2. **It** determines which operations   (l. 9) ....
3. **These two units** are made up of   (l. 15) ....
4. **that** can be in one of two states   (l. 16) ....
5. **that** directs the sequence   (l. 20) ....
6. **in which** the actual arithmetic operations   (l. 25) ....
7. **It** also performs some kind of   (l. 27) ....
8. **on which** the control unit and the arithmetic-logical unit operate   (l. 30) ....
9. **where** manual control operations   (l. 34) ....
10. **It** is used mainly when the computer   (l. 36) ....

Unit 9 The Central Processing Unit

5 Understanding words

Refer back to the text and find synonyms for the following words.

1. specific   (l. 7)   ....
2. decides   (l. 9)   ....
3. job   (l. 18) ....
4. movement   (l. 22) ....
5. situated   (l. 31) ....

Now refer back to the text and find antonyms for the following words.

6. exceptional (l. 1)   ....
7. generally   (l. 2)   ....
8. not needed   (l. 26) ....
9. taken out   (l. 33) ....
10. shut down   (l. 37) ....

6 Word forms

First choose the appropriate form of the words to complete the sentences. Then check the differences of meaning in your dictionary.

1. function, functional, functionally
   a. Learning to program is a .... part of any course in computer science.
   b. The central processing unit has many ....
   c. In order for the computer to .... properly, there should be no fluctuation in the electric current.

2. sequence, sequential, sequentially
   a. The control unit of the CPU directs the .... operations of the system.
   b. Data must be presented .... to the processor unless the computer is programmed otherwise.
   c. A program must be a detailed account of the .... the processor must follow to solve the problem.

3. logic, logical, logically
   a. To be a good programmer, one must be .... in ones approach to a problem.
   b. The .... operations performed by the arithmetic-logical unit are under the control of the control unit.
   c. A program must be .... organized if successful results are to be obtained.

4. connection, connect, connected, connective
   a. On-line equipment is usually .... to the computer.
   b. Malfunctioning equipment can often be traced to a bad electrical ....
   c. Whether one is writing computer science related information or not, the use of .... is very important.

5. computer, compute, computerized, computed, computation
   a. The banking industry has become more and more ....
   b. It is a fact that humans cannot .... as fast as ....
   c. The .... requirements necessary to produce the payroll for a large company take a very long time.

7 Content review

Use the texts you have studied so far to complete the following table.

SYSTEM	SUBSYSTEMS	PARTS	FUNCTIONS
Computer	Input devices		
	Processor	Memory	
			1. 2. 3. 4.
		Arithmetic	1. 2.
	Output devices		

FOCUS G

Time sequence

In Focus E we looked at some of the markers used for enumerating the order in which things are to be said when making lists or giving instructions. However, it didn't mention those markers which outline the *time sequence* in which events occur. It is equally important to recognize the sequence of events, especially in such activities as scheduling, recounting historical facts, doing routine activities and conducting and describing experiments.

As we know, events do not simply occur, they occur either before, during or after other events. This time sequence may be chronological, logical or causal. Once a time-reference has been established, certain adjectives and adverbials may order subsequent information in relation to it. The following tables are examples of time relaters.

Table 1

Previous to given time-references, i.e. **before**

	TIME RELATERS		
Adjectives	earlier former	preceeding previous	
Adverbials	already prior before	earlier first formerly	previously so far yet
	before that before then	up to now/then until now/then	in the beginning (long) ago

Examples
1. The memory storage capacity of **earlier** computers was not as large as those of today.
2. When the first digital computer was developed, the first analog computer had **already** been in use for some time.
3. **Up to now**, computers have not created too much unemployment.

Table 2

Simultaneous with given time-reference, i.e. **during**

	TIME RELATERS	
Adjectives	contemporary	simultaneous
Adverbials	at present at this point now today for the time being at the moment	meantime meanwhile in the meantime when at the same time

Examples
1. Computers might be used in the future as **simultaneous** translating machines.
2. **At present**, computers are used for printing newspapers.
3. In the future, computers will probably replace most of our daily activities, but **in the meantime** scientists are still trying to develop computers to their full potential.

Subsequent to time-reference, i.e. **after**

	TIME RELATERS		
Adjectives	following	later	next
Adverbials	afterwards after that eventually	since since then by the time	by the end soon next

Examples
1. **Since** the development of the chip, computers have become cheaper and more compact.
2. You should have a good basic understanding of computers **by the time** you finish this reading course.
3. After the development of transistors, the **later** computers were much faster.

N.B. Time sequence is also shown by the different verb tenses.

Examples
1. Vannevar Bush **had built** the first analog computer long before Professor Aiken and some men at IBM **invented** the first digital computer.
2. At the rate computer technology **is growing**, computers, as we **know** them today, **will** soon **become** obsolete.

Focus G Time sequence

Sample paragraph

Computers, as we know them **today**, haven't been around for a long time. It wasn't **until** the mid-1940s that the first working digital computer was completed. But **since then**, computers have evolved tremendously. Vacuum tubes were used in the first-generation computers only to be replaced by transistors in the second-generation computers **at the beginning** of the 1960s. **By the end** of the 1960s, transistors were replaced by tiny integrated circuit boards and, consequently, a new generation of computers was on the market. Fourth-generation computers are **now** produced with circuits that are much smaller than **before** and fit on a single chip. **Soon** fifth-generation computers will be produced, and these will no doubt be better than their predecessors.

Exercise

Read the following paragraph and as you read, underline the time relaters.

There are some who say that computers have a very short history but, because they are machines that manipulate numbers, others disagree. More than 5000 years ago, a need to count was recognized, and somebody had the idea of using first his fingers, then pebbles to keep track of the count. History is not clear as to whether the need was recognized before or after the idea occurred. Since that time, the abacus was invented and some form of it was used well into the 16th century. During the 17th and 18th centuries many easy ways of calculating were devised. Logarithm tables, calculus and the basis for the modern slide rule were born out of that period of time. It was not until the early 1800s that the first calculating machine appeared and not too long after, Charles Babbage designed a machine which became the basis for building today's computers. A hundred years later the first analog computer was built, but the first digital computer was not completed until 1944. Since then computers have gone through four generations from digital computers using vacuum tubes in the 1950s, transistors in the early 1960s, integrated in the mid-60s, and a single chip in the 1970s. At the rate computer technology is growing now, we can expect more changes in this field by the end of this decade.

UNIT 10

The Control Unit and the Arithmetic-Logical Unit

[1] The basic components of a computer system, the input, the output, the memory, and the processor operate only in response to commands from the control unit. The control unit operates by reading one instruction at a time from memory and taking the action called for by each instruction. In this way it controls the flow between main storage and the **arithmetic-logical unit**.

[2] A control unit has the following components:
  a. A **counter** that selects the instructions, one at a time, from memory.
  b. A **register** that temporarily holds the instruction read from memory while it is being executed.
  c. A **decoder** that takes the coded instruction and breaks it down into the individual commands necessary to carry it out.
  d. A **clock**, which, while not a clock in the sense of a time-keeping device, does produce marks at regular intervals. These timing marks are electronic and very rapid.

[3] **Binary arithmetic** (the kind of arithmetic the computer uses), the logical operations and some special functions are performed by the **arithmetic-logical unit**. The primary components of the ALU are banks of bi-stable devices, which are called **registers**. Their purpose is to hold the numbers involved in the calculation and to hold the results temporarily until they can be transferred to memory. At the core of the arithmetic-logical unit is a very high-speed binary adder, which is used to carry out at least the four basic arithmetic functions (addition, subtraction, multiplication, and division). Typical modern computers can perform as many as one hundred thousand additions of pairs of thirty-two-bit binary numbers within a second. The logical unit consists of electronic circuitry which compares information and makes decisions based upon the results of the comparison. The decisions that can be made are whether a number is greater than ($>$), equal to ($=$), or less than ($<$) another number.

Unit 10 The Control Unit and the Arithmetic-Logical Unit

Exercises

1 Main idea

Which statement does *not* express the main idea of the text?

☐ 1. The control unit coordinates all the activities of a computer.

☐ 2. The arithmetic-logical unit cannot function without the control unit.

☐ 3. The arithmetic-logical unit is the most important component of a computer.

2 Understanding the passage

Indicate whether the following ideas are stated or not stated (S/NS) in the text.

S   NS

☐ ☐ 1. The basic components of a computer cannot operate without commands from the control unit.

☐ ☐ 2. Programs and data on which the control unit and the arithmetic-logical unit operate must be in internal memory in order to be processed.

☐ ☐ 3. The control unit and the arithmetic-logical unit are part of the processor.

☐ ☐ 4. The control unit directs the movement of information between the arithmetic-logical unit and main storage.

☐ ☐ 5. Binary arithmetic is not performed by the control unit.

☐ ☐ 6. There are more components to the arithmetic-logical unit than to the control unit.

☐ ☐ 7. The arithmetic-logical unit does not always transfer the results immediately to memory.

☐ ☐ 8. The arithmetic unit and the logical unit do not perform the same types of operations.

☐ ☐ 9. The logical unit can decide whether a number is equal to, greater than or less than another number.

☐ ☐ 10. Without the decision-making function, a computer would simply be a large adding machine.

3 Locating information

Find the passages in the text where the following ideas are expressed. Give the line references.

.... 1. Registers are the most important parts of the arithmetic-logical unit.
.... 2. The logical unit is responsible for comparing numbers.
.... 3. Modern computers can perform hundreds of thousands of additions in a second.
.... 4. The arithmetic unit does all the necessary calculations.
.... 5. The control unit has many different components with different functions.
.... 6. The basic computer components can only respond to commands from the control unit.
.... 7. The arithmetic unit can store results for a short time if necessary.

4 Contextual reference

Look back at the text and find out what the words in **bold** typeface refer to.

1. **In this way** it controls the flow (l. 5) ....
2. In this way **it** controls the flow (l. 5) ....
3. **that** temporarily holds the instruction (l. 10) ....
4. while **it** is being executed (l. 11) ....
5. necessary to carry **it** out (l. 13) ....
6. **which** while not a clock (l. 14) ....
7. **Their** purpose is to hold (l. 20) ....
8. until **they** can be transferred (l. 22) ....
9. **which** is used to carry out (l. 23) ....
10. **which** compares information (l. 28) ....

5 Understanding words

Refer back to the text and find synonyms for the following words.

1. orders (l. 2) ....
2. one after another (l. 8) ....
3. for a short time (l. 10) ....
4. time period (l. 15) ....

Now refer back to the text and find antonyms for the following words.

5. together (l. 8) ....
6. build up (l. 12) ....
7. haphazard (l. 15) ....

6 Word forms

First choose the appropriate form of the words to complete the sentences. Then check the differences of meaning in your dictionary.

1. response, respond, responded, responding
    a. The arithmetic-logical unit .... to commands from the control unit.
    b. The components of a computer system operate only in .... to commands from the control unit.

2. decision, decide, decided, decidedly
    a. The .... to continue space exploration will cause a lot of expense.
    b. A programmer .... what the computer is to do, and without the program the computer cannot process the necessary information.
    c. It cannot be .... yet what success fibre optics will have in computer technology.

3. distinguishing, distinguish, distinguishable, distinguished
    a. A comma is not easily .... from a period on a small CRT.
    b. Computers have many .... characteristics that the layman is unaware of.
    c. An experienced programmer can .... between a Cobol statement and a Basic statement.

4. notice, noticed, noticeable, noticeably
    a. Although computers are manufactured in different countries, it is difficult to .... any differences in the way they are designed.
    b. There should be a .... improvement in your English at this point in the course.

5. provision, provide, provided, provider
    a. A programmer must .... the computer with the necessary data and instructions to execute the problem.
    b. The .... of a new and larger computer installation will result in a better service to customers.
    c. A programmer can operate a computer .... he has the proper training.

7a Content review

Match the words in column A with the words or statements in column B.

A	B
☐ 1. counter	a. does the calculations necessary to solve the problem
☐ 2. register	b. temporarily hold results before transferring to memory
☐ 3. decoder	c. temporarily holds the instructions
☐ 4. clock	d. does the decision-making operations
☐ 5. binary arithmetic	e. produces timing marks
☐ 6. control unit	f. does the calculations and makes decisions to solve problems
☐ 7. arithmetic unit	g. directs movement of information between memory and arithmetic unit
☐ 8. logic unit	h. breaks down the coded information to be handled
☐ 9. registers	i. based on 0 and 1
☐ 10. arithmetic-logical unit	j. chooses the instructions

7b Content review

Use the information in the text to complete the table.

	PARTS	FUNCTIONS
Control Unit	1.	*selects*
	2.	*holds*
	3.	*breaks down*
	4.	*produces*
Arithmetic Logical Unit	1.	*hold*
	2.	*carries out*
	3.	*and* 1. 2. = *another number* 3.

FOCUS H

Giving examples

Using examples to explain a point or to illustrate an idea is commonly used in texts when the primary objective is to teach the reader about some subject. It is thus important to differentiate between the idea or ideas presented, and the illustration of the idea, with examples.

Writers often say *explicitly* which things are examples by using the connectives in the table below.

for example	examples of	shown by
for instance	instances of	exemplifies
an example of this	cases of	shows
as an example	illustrations of	illustrates
that is	exemplified by	a second/third
such as	illustrated by	example etc.
like	seen in	namely

Sample sentences with examples in italics:

1. The switches, like the cores, are capable of being in one of two possible states **that is**, *on or off; magnetized or unmagnetized*.
2. Computers have circuits for performing arithmetic operations **such as**: *addition, subtraction, division, multiplication* and *exponentiation*.
3. The computer can only decide three things, **namely**: *Is one number less than another?, Are two numbers equal?,* and *Is one number greater than another?*
4. Computers can process information at extremely rapid rates; **for example**, they can solve certain arithmetic problems *millions of times faster than a skilled mathematician*.
5. Using the very limited capabilities possessed by all computers, *the task of producing a university payroll*, **for instance**, can be done quite easily.

N.B.   Sometimes the markers *follow* the examples, separated by commas.

Not all texts present examples explicitly, some exemplifications are given *implicitly*, in which case, the above markers are not used.

Example

Some of the most common methods of inputting information is to use *punched cards*, *magnetic tape*, *disks* and *terminals*. The computer's input device, which might be a *card reader*, a *tape drive* or *disk drive*, depending on the medium used, reads the information into the computer. For outputting information, two common devices used are a *printer*, which prints the new information on paper, or a *CRT display screen*, which shows the results on a T.V.-like screen.

Exercise 1

Using the example paragraph above, label the diagram.

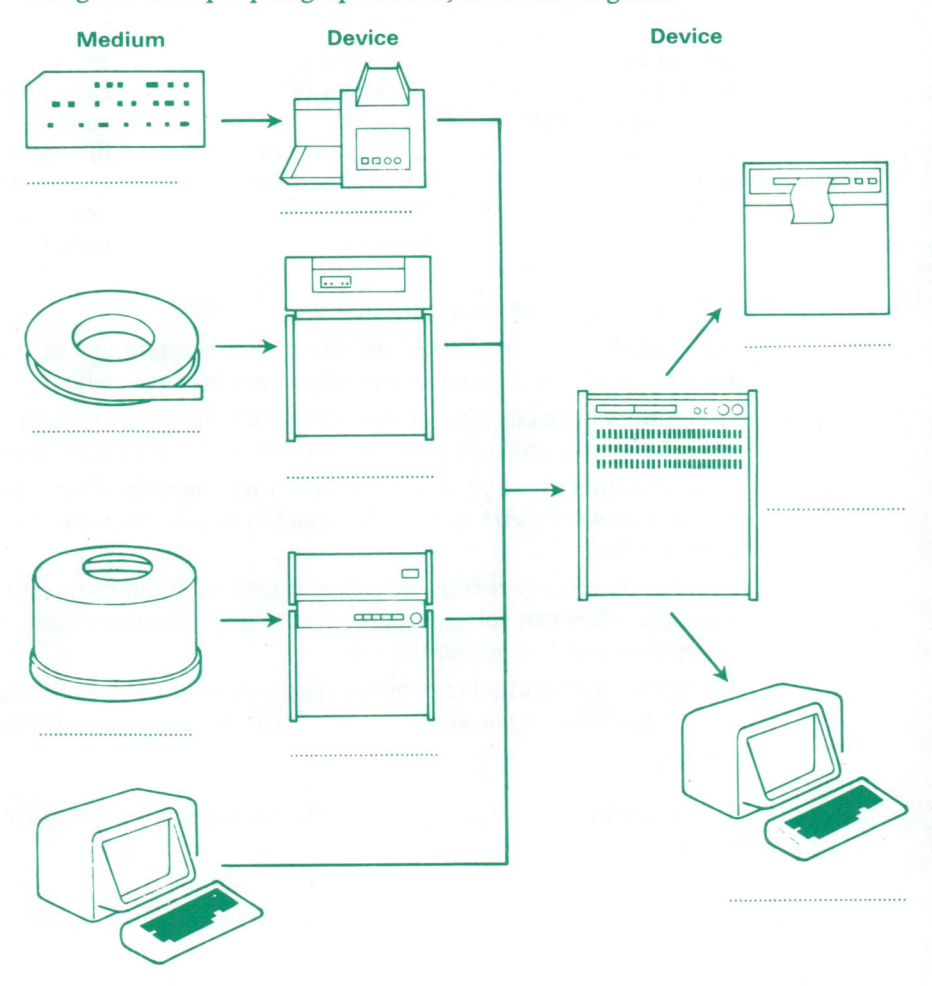

Focus H Giving examples

Exercise 2

Fill in the missing information in the following text by referring to the diagram in Exercise 1.

Input devices such as ...., ...
.... and .... are used for reading information into the computer. .... and .... are examples of output devices.

Exercise 3

Refer back to paragraph 3 and 4 of the text on 'Microcomputers' (Unit 8) to complete the table below.

PARA	MARKER	ILLUSTRATION OF IDEA	IDEA
[3]		robots	
[4]			'a one shot deal'

Now refer back to paragraph 5 and 6 of the text on 'The Central Processing Unit' (Unit 9) to complete the table below.

PARA	MARKER	ILLUSTRATION OF IDEA	IDEA
[5]	namely		logical operations
[6]		disks or tapes	

SECTION 5

Memory

UNIT 11

Primary and secondary memory

[1] The term 'memory' is usually used to refer to the **internal storage** locations of a computer. It is also called **real storage** or **primary memory**, and is expressed as quantities of K. For example, computers are advertised as having memories of 16K or 152K, depending on their storage capacity. Each K is equal to 1,024 **bytes**, and each byte is equal to 8 **bits**.

[2] Primary memory is closely associated with the CPU because it stores programs and data temporarily, thus making them immediately available for processing by the CPU. To facilitate processing, two things are needed: **random access** and speed. The former means that any part of the memory may be read, or **accessed**, equally quickly. This is made possible by the system of **addresses** in primary memory, where the storage locations are like a series of tiny compartments, each having its own address. These addresses are like the addresses of houses, in that they do not change. Because they are always fixed, the control unit knows where to find them at a very high speed. When it finds them, it puts into the compartments whatever must go there and wipes out whatever was stored there. The information present in these compartments is called the **contents** of the memory.

[3] Most primary memory is costly, and therefore it is used transiently, which means that a program, or parts of it, is kept in internal storage while the program is being executed. This, however, is not true for mini and micro applications where the computer performs the same function, referred to as a **dedicated function**, all the time. But since computers must process vast quantities of data and programs, a lot of storage space is required. For this reason various secondary memory technologies have been developed.

[4] Secondary memory devices fall into two categories: **sequential devices** and **random-access** devices. Sequential devices permit information to be written on to or read off some storage medium in a fixed sequence only. In order to get at a particular data item, it is necessary to pass over all the data preceding it. An example of such a device is the **magnetic tape**. Its cost is low, but access to specified data may take a considerable length of time. On the other hand, random-access devices are designed to permit direct, or almost direct, access to specified data. These devices bypass large quantities of irrelevant data and therefore reduce access

time considerably. An example of this technology is the magnetic disk, which is faster than the magnetic tape and also more expensive. When disks are hooked up to the computer and used as an extension of internal storage in order to increase the capacity of primary memory, this is called **virtual storage**. For example, a computer with 256K bytes of real storage may seem to have 512K bytes of virtual storage by using disks to provide additional storage.

Exercises

1 Main idea

Which statement best expresses the main idea of the text? Why did you eliminate the other choices?

☐ 1. There are two types of memory: primary and secondary.

☐ 2. Primary memory is more important than secondary memory.

☐ 3. Secondary memory devices are unimportant in a computer system.

2 Understanding the passage

Indicate whether the following ideas were stated or not stated (S/NS) in the text.

S   NS

☐ ☐ 1. The term 'memory' can be expressed in other ways.

☐ ☐ 2. Computers are often advertised according to their memory capacity.

☐ ☐ 3. The CPU can easily access information from internal storage.

☐ ☐ 4. Minicomputers and microcomputers have a similar memory capacity.

☐ ☐ 5. The control unit needs to know the location where information is stored or needs to be stored.

☐ ☐ 6. Primary memory is more expensive than secondary memory.

☐ ☐ 7. There are two types of secondary memory device.

☐ ☐ 8. Information stored on magnetic disk can be retrieved faster than if that same information were on tape.

☐ ☐ 9. Disks and tapes can be stored in a library.

☐ ☐ 10. Computers can process information even if complete programs are not put in internal storage.

Unit 11 *Primary and secondary memory* 113

3 Locating information

Find the passages in the text where the following ideas are expressed. Give the line references.

.... 1. Speed and random access are important in processing information.
.... 2. Random-access devices are more efficient than sequential devices.
.... 3. The CPU and primary memory work closely together.
.... 4. Virtual storage increases the memory capacity of a computer.
.... 5. Real storage, internal storage, and primary memory are all the same.
.... 6. Information is stored in memory in compartments with a specific location.
.... 7. There are two classes of secondary memory device.
.... 8. Only parts of programs are kept in primary storage while a program is being run through.

4 Contextual reference

Look back at the text and find out what the words in **bold** typeface refer to.

1. **It** is also called (*l. 2*) ....
2. depending on **their** storage capacity (*l. 4*) ....
3. thus making **them** (*l. 8*) ....
4. **The former** means that (*l. 10*) ....
5. **where** the storage locations (*l. 12*) ....
6. **each** having its own address (*l. 13*) ....
7. in that **they** do not change (*l. 15*) ....
8. where to find **them** (*l. 16*) ....
9. whatever must go **there** (*l. 17*) ....
10. or parts of **it** (*l. 21*) ....

5 Understanding words

Refer back to the text and find synonyms for the following words.

1. represented (*l. 3*) ....
2. erases (*l. 17*) ....
3. carried out (*l. 22*) ....
4. before (*l. 32*) ....
5. very much (*l. 37*) ....

Now refer back to the text and find antonyms for the following words.

6. latter (*l. 10*) ....
7. disallow (*l. 29*) ....

8. unnecessary   (l. 31) ....
9. go through   (l. 36) ....
10. imaginary   (l. 42) ....

6 Word forms

First choose the appropriate form of the words to complete the sentences. Then check the differences of meaning in your dictionary.

1. expression, expressive, express, expressed
   a. Information sent via a computer is faster than using the .... system of airlines or postal services.
   b. An .... such as 'He or she has a computer for a brain' means that he or she is a fast-thinking person.
   c. Computers understand commands .... in the form of 0 and 1.

2. equality, equal, equally, equalize
   a. The symbol ≠ means that two things are not ....
   b. A microcomputer doesn't .... a minicomputer in flexibility.
   c. The two computer languages Pascal and PL1 are .... difficult.

3. consideration, consider, considerable, considerably
   a. There is a .... difference between written and spoken English.
   b. It is important to .... the capabilities and limitations of a computer before buying one.
   c. New printers can print results .... faster than previously.

4. design, designed, designation, designer, designing
   a. Due to the advances in computer technology, computer .... are faced with a more challenging job.
   b. Computers are .... to process information accurately and quickly.
   c. Computer architects are constantly trying to improve on the .... of computers.

5. advertisement, advertise, advertised
   a. There are many computer-related jobs .... in *The New York Times*.
   b. The Computer Center will soon .... for more operators and programmers.

c. Career opportunities in computer science and related fields can usually be found in the .... section of newspapers.

7 Content review

Match the words in column A with the words or statements in column B.

A	B
☐ 1. internal storage	a. means any part of memory can be read equally quickly
☐ 2. real storage	
☐ 3. random access	b. the information contained in the storage locations
☐ 4. addresses	
☐ 5. contents	c. are storage locations in internal storage
☐ 6. sequential access	
☐ 7. virtual storage	d. refers to memory
	e. hooking up secondary memory devices onto memory to increase their capacity
	f. sometimes called primary memory
	g. information must be read from secondary memory devices in a fixed pattern

8 Focus review

Focus H Giving examples

Complete the following table by referring back to the text on 'Primary and Secondary Memory'.

PARA	ITEM(S) TO BE EXEMPLIFIED	EXAMPLE MARKER	EXAMPLE
[1]	*quantities of K*		
[4] a.		*an example*	
[4] b.			*magnetic disk*
[4] c.	*virtual storage*		

FOCUS 1

Adding information

There are many reasons why people read; but in an academic setting, reading is primarily done to get information on a particular subject. It is important to the reader to understand the relationship between the information given and the information which preceded it. Often information is presented in such a way as to suggest a *reinforcement* of what has been said, or to show a *similarity* to what has been said before.

When writers give explanations about something, they usually offer examples to support their argument in favour of a particular viewpoint. They may choose to present the information *deductively*, in which case a generalization is given first and then examples are given in support of the general statement or principle. Others prefer to provide examples first, and then make the generalization. This form of presentation is *inductive*.

1 Reinforcement

The markers used to show *reinforcement*, whether in deductive or inductive organization, are:

furthermore	too	what is more
in addition	moreover	also*
as well as	additionally	again*
besides		

* occurs in initial position

Examples
1. **In addition** to their speed, computers are accurate and can do repetitive operations over and over again without becoming tired or bored.
2. Microcomputers are cheaper than mainframes, **as well as** being compact and portable.

Focus I Adding information

2 Similarity

Markers used to add information to show that it is *similar* to what was said before are:

equally*	similarly
likewise	correspondingly
in the same way	

* occurs in initial position

Examples
1. Microcomputers can have a storage capacity of up to 32K; **likewise** minicomputers.
2. Many minicomputers are used merely for a fixed application and run only a single program. Microcomputers operate **in much the same way** as is the case in automobile emission control systems.

Other markers or connectives used to add information explicitly, in the form of either reinforcement or similarity, are:

another
other additional
further

Exercise 1

While reading the following text, circle the markers used to add information and underline the information that is being added.

Microcomputer technology is already being applied in areas that only a decade ago were impossible. One of these areas is in medicine and its related fields. For example, severely handicapped people with cerebral palsy, who have very little limb control, can now use the Blissterm, a computerized version of the 500-symbol Bliss system. Because of their handicap, these people can hear but can't respond. Now, with the Blissterm, it is possible to extend their skills.

In addition to the Blissterm, other devices have been designed to aid the handicapped who are confined to wheel-chairs and have no control, or virtually no control, of their limbs. A special microcomputer that responds to eye movement has been developed which, when attached to a wheelchair's mechanism, allows the person to move about independently. By opening and closing the eyes and blinking, the person can make the wheelchair start or stop; and when the eyes move left or right, so does the wheelchair. Similarly, there are other devices that have been developed to help severely handicapped people employ the limited use of their fingers or toes to type. Furthermore, such people

Focus I Adding information

can now type with their eyes, by simply focusing on the letter to be typed. Attached to the eyeglasses is a small device that responds to the eye and transmits the signal to a typewriter. It takes time to write a letter this way, but it's better than not being able to write at all.

Again, another example of electronic development in computer technology, that has opened vast opportunities for the blind, is the voice box. Until now, people with heavily restricted vision have had to rely on Braille or sighted people to pick out mistakes on the computer screens or printouts. Now, errors shown on the screen are duplicated audibly through a voice synthesizer. This new simpler voice correction system is a boon to all visually-handicapped students, because computers are now being used more and more as an educational aid.

Exercise 2

Complete the following table by referring back to Unit 3, paragraph 5; Unit 6, paragraph 2; Unit 8, paragraph 1, and Unit 8, paragraph 4.

UNIT PARA	INFORMATION	MARKER	ADDITIONAL INFORMATION	TYPE OF ADDITION
3 [5]	*expensive to run*			
6 [2]		*moreover*		
8 [1]			*minicomputers up to 32 bits*	
8 [4]				*reinforcement*

UNIT 12

Types of memory

[1] As mentioned previously, one of the most important characteristics of a computer is its capability of storing information in its memory long enough to process it. Not all computers have the same type of memory. In this section, three types of memory will be discussed: **core** memory, **semiconductor** memory (or chip), and **bubble** memory.

[2] The memory of the first computers was made up of a kind of grid of fine vertical and horizontal wires. At each intersection where the wires crossed, there was a small ferrite ring called a core (hence the name 'core memory') which was capable of being either magnetized or demagnetized. Every intersection had its unique address; consequently, when an electrical current was passed through the wires, the magnetized as well as the unmagnetized cores were identified by their respective addresses. Each core represented a binary digit of either 0 or 1, depending on its state. Early computers had a capacity of around 80,000 bits; whereas now, it is not surprising to hear about computers with a memory capacity of millions of bits. This has been made possible by the advent of transistors and by the advances in the manufacture of miniaturized circuitry. As a result, mainframes have been reduced in both size and cost. Throughout the 1950s, 1960s and up to the mid-1970s, core memory dominated the market.

[3] In the 1970s, there was a further development which revolutionized the computer field. This was the ability to etch thousands of integrated circuits onto a tiny piece (chip) of silicon, which is a non-metallic element with semiconductor characteristics. Chips have thousands of identical circuits, each one capable of storing one bit. Because of the very small size of the chip, and consequently of the circuits etched on it, electrical signals do not have to travel far; hence, they are transmitted faster. Moreover, the size of the components containing the circuitry can be considerably reduced, a step which has led to the introduction of both minis and micros. As a result, computers have become smaller, faster, and cheaper. There is one problem with semiconductor memory, however: when power is removed, information in the memory is lost – unlike core memory, which is capable of retaining information during a power failure.

[4] Another development in the field of computer memories is bubble memory. The concept consists of creating a thin film of metallic alloys over the memory board. When this film is magnetized, it produces magnetic bubbles, the presence or absence of which represents one bit of information. These bubbles are extremely tiny, about 0.1 micrometer in diameter. Therefore, a magnetic bubble memory can store information at a greater density than existing memories, which makes it suitable for micros. Bubble memories are not expensive, consume little power, are small in size, and are highly reliable. There is probably a lot more to learn about them, and research in this field continues.

Exercises

1 Main idea

Which statements do **not** express the main idea of the text?

☐ 1. Core memory was the first type of computer memory developed.

☐ 2. There are at least three different kinds of memory used in computers.

☐ 3. Bubble memory is the latest development in computer memory.

2 Understanding the passage

Decide whether the following statements are true or false (T/F) by referring to the information in the text. Then make the necessary changes so that the false statements become true.

T   F

☐ ☐ 1. The most important function of a computer is to hold information in its memory in order to process it.

☐ ☐ 2. Minicomputers, microcomputers, and mainframes all have the same kind of memory.

☐ ☐ 3. Semiconductor memory was developed before core memory and after bubble memory.

☐ ☐ 4. Core memory uses small metal rings which can be magnetized or unmagnetized.

☐ ☐ 5. The state of the core can be represented by either 0 or 1.

☐ ☐ 6. Early computer memories had less storage capacity than newer ones.

☐ ☐ 7. A transistor and a chip are the same kind of device.

Unit 12 *Types of memory* 121

T	F	
☐	☐	8. The development of chips made it possible for minicomputers and microcomputers to be invented.
☐	☐	9. Bubble memory is smaller than a chip.
☐	☐	10. Bubble memory doesn't have very many advantages.

3 Locating information

Find the passages in the text where the following ideas are expressed. Give the line references.

.... 1. First there is core memory.
.... 2. Further to this development, chips evolved.
.... 3. There are three types of memory.
.... 4. This consists of producing a thin film over a memory board.
.... 5. Then semiconductor memory was developed.
.... 6. There is still a lot to learn about this process.
.... 7. This is made up of thin wires and rings.
.... 8. Finally, bubble memory was invented.

4 Contextual reference

Look back at the text and find out what the words in **bold** typeface refer to.

1. long enough to process **it** (l. 3) ....
2. **where** the wires crossed (l. 7) ....
3. **which** was capable of being (l. 9) ....
4. by **their** respective addresses (l. 12) ....
5. **This** has been made possible (l. 16) ....
6. **which** revolutionized the computer field (l. 21) ....
7. **each one** capable of storing one bit (l. 25) ....
8. of the circuits etched on **it** (l. 26) ....
9. **it** produces magnetic bubbles (l. 37) ....
10. **of which** represents one bit (l. 38) ....

5 Understanding words

Refer back to the text and find synonyms for the following words.

1. said (l. 1) ....
2. own (l. 12) ....
3. progress (l. 17) ....
4. keeping (l. 33) ....
5. appropriate (l. 42) ....

Now refer back to the text and find antonyms for the following words.

6. neither .... nor (l. 9) ....
7. bypassed (l. 11) ....
8. increased (l. 18) ....
9. not producing (l. 36) ....
10. don't use up (l. 42) ....

6 Word forms

First choose the appropriate form of the words to complete the sentences. Then check the differences of meaning in your dictionary.

1. alteration, alter, altered
   a. When a program doesn't work properly, it is often necessary to make .... to it.
   b. The omission of data from a program can .... its results drastically.
   c. The use of the computer in business has .... the workload of many people.

2. electricity, electric, electrical, electrically
   a. A lot of .... is needed to operate large computer systems.
   b. Alexander Graham Bell invented the .... light bulb.
   c. Many students today are studying to become .... engineers.

3. reduction, reduce, reduced
   a. The introduction of the computer in the workplace has .... the workload of many people.
   b. There will probably be a great .... in the consumption of oil in the next decade due to the use of computer technology.

4. creation, create, created, creative
   a. A programmer usually has a .... as well as a logical mind.
   b. It takes a lot of inspiration and hard work to come up with a new .... in computer technology.
   c. Computers have certainly .... new opportunities for fraud.

Unit 12 Types of memory

7 Content review

Use the information in the text on 'Types of Memory' to complete the table.

TYPE	DEVELOPED	SIZE	COMPOSITION	MEMORY CAPACITY
1.		large		80,000 bits
2.			integrated circuits on non-metallic element	
3.				

8 Focus review

Focus G   Time sequence

Complete the following table by referring back to the text on 'Types of Memory'.

PARA	TIME SEQUENCE MARKER	INFORMATION
[2]	The computer	had memories made up of a kind of grid of fine vertical and horizontal wires
[2]	computers	had a capacity of around 80,000 bits
[2]	whereas	it is not surprising to hear about computers with a memory capacity of millions of bits
[2]		core memory dominated the market
[3]		there was further development which revolutionized the computer field

Focus I   Adding information

Complete the following sentences by referring back to the text on 'Types of Memory'.

1. In the 1970s, there was a .... development which revolutionized the computer field. (Para. 3)
2. ...., the size of the components containing the circuitry can be considerably reduced ... (Para. 3)
3. .... development in the field of computer memories is bubble memory. (Para. 4)

FOCUS J

Giving an explanation or a definition

In texts similar to those in this book, authors often give *definitions* to new or unfamiliar terms, or vocabulary items and concepts, or ideas specific to the subject being discussed. Not only are definitions given, but *explanations* are often supplied, either implicitly or explicitly, to avoid confusion in the mind of the reader.

1 Some expressions or markers used to define or explain a statement explicitly are:

means	by ... we mean*
is taken to be	by ... is meant*
denotes	in other words
refers to	that is (to say)*
is defined as	
*occurs in initial position	

Examples
1. The term computer **refers to** the processor plus the internal memory.
2. A chip **is defined as** a tiny square piece of silicon upon which several layers of an integrated circuit are etched or imprinted, after which the circuit is encapsulated in plastic, ceramic, or metal.
3. **By** peripherals **we mean** those devices which are attached to the computer.

2 There are other methods used to define or explain, depending on the style used. One very common method is to give the term being defined and say what it is without repeating the term, i.e. X is/are Y.

Examples
1. A computer **is an electronic device**.
2. Tapes and disks **are memory devices**.
3. Printers **are output devices**.

3 Another very common method is to use the same pattern as in 2 above and also give some distinguishing characteristics.

Examples

1. A computer is an electronic device **which/that processes information**.
2. Tapes and disks are memory devices **which/that can be stored away for future use**.
3. A programmer is a person **who prepares programs to solve problems**.

N.B. The relative pronouns used in this type of definition or explanation will be **who** or **that** for people, **when** for a period of time, **where** for a place or location, and **that** or **which** for things.

4 One of the most frequent forms of definition or explanation is to use two nouns (or noun phrases) in apposition, separated by commas.

Examples

1. Computers, **electronic devices for processing information,** are now used in practically every aspect of life.
2. Systems software, **programs,** direct the computer to perform tasks.
3. Turnkey systems, **complete hardware/software products,** may be provided along with the hardware by a systems supplier.

Exercise 1

Study the following definitions. A definition usually includes all three parts: the term to be defined, the group it belongs to, and the characteristics which distinguish it from other members of the group.

TERM	GROUP	CHARACTERISTICS
A core	is a ferrite ring	which is capable of being either magnetized or demagnetized
Silicon	is a nonmetallic element	with semiconductor characteristics

Now analyse the following definitions and identify the different parts by circling the term; by underlining the group once, and by underlining the characteristics twice.

1. A computer is a machine with an intricate network of electronic circuits that operate switches or magnetize tiny metal cores. (Unit 1)
2. An abacus is a bead frame in which the beads are moved from left to right. (Unit 2)

3. Input is the information presented to the computer. (Unit 3)
4. The term 'computer' includes those parts of hardware in which calculations and other data manipulations are performed, and the high-speed interval memory in which data and calculations are stored during actual executions of programs. (Unit 3)
5. A 'system' is a good mixture of integrated parts working together to form a useful whole. (Unit 5)
6. Large computer systems, or mainframes, as they are referred to in the field of computer science, are those computer systems found in computer installations processing immense amounts of data. (Unit 6)
7. Although there is no exact definition for a minicomputer, it is generally understood to refer to a computer whose mainframe is physically small, has a fixed word length between 8 and 32 bits, and costs less than $100,000 for the central processor. (Unit 7)

Exercise 2 Giving an explanation
Complete the following table by referring back to the text on 'Primary and Secondary Memory' (Unit 11).

LINE	TERM	EXPLANATION MARKER	EXPLANATION
1	*Memory*		
10		means	
13			*a series of tiny compartments each having its own address.*
14	*These addresses*		
21		*which means*	
23			*computer performs the same function.*

Focus J Giving an explanation or a definition

Exercise 3 Giving a definition

Complete the following table by referring back to the appropriate units and paragraphs as indicated in the table.

UNIT [PARA]	TERM	GROUP	CHARACTERISTICS
1 [2]	computers		
2 [5]		silicon	
3 [1]			electronically processed by computers
5 [4]	turnkey systems		
6 [2]			can simulate, imitate different measurements, by electric means
7 [1]		semiconductor device	
9 [5]	ALU		
10 [3]		bi-stable devices	
11 [1]			expresses as quantities of K

SECTION 6

Input and output devices

UNIT 13

Cards and card readers

[1] An essential requirement for making good use of computers is the ability to put information into the machine. Until the early 1960s, one of the most frequently used devices for providing input data to a computer was the **punched card**, a major storage medium for computer programs and data. Most people are very surprised to find that punched cards were used as long ago as 1780 on textile machinery. However, the first application of punched cards for the representation of large quantities of data was made by Dr Herman Hollerith in 1890. Working for the US Census Bureau, he realized that unless some means of speeding up the analysis of census data were found, it would take more than ten years to complete the job. He recognized the value of the punched cards for this purpose, devised a code for representing data on the cards, and invented the necessary machines to meet his needs. Dr Hollerith went on to found a company to produce these machines, which in 1924 became International Business Machines, or IBM for short.

[2] The use of punched cards actually requires two separate pieces of equipment. The first is a **keypunch**, which looks like a large typewriter and is not physically connected to the computer in any way. Hence, it is said to be **off-line**. The second is a **card reader** which, as its name implies, reads the information from the card. Unlike the keypunch, it is connected to the computer and is, therefore, said to be **on-line**.

[3] The most commonly used card has rectangular punches to record data (see Figure 13.1), although one major manufacturer uses circular punches. The reason for one corner of a card being cut off is so that the user has a reference point in placing the cards in the card reader. When a typist or **keypunch operator** presses a key, which is labelled with a character, i.e. a letter, number, or some special character, the machine punches a number of holes in one column of the card. The card is organized into 12 rows and 80 columns. For this reason the character is changed into a 12-bit word which is represented by writing the holes as 1 and the unpunched areas as 0. Because most cards have 80 columns, no more than 80 characters can be punched on one card. These columns are numbered from left to right, but the rows are numbered top to bottom as follows: 12, 11, 10 (or 0), 1, 2, 3, 4, 5, 6, 7, 8, 9. The top three rows are called **punch** rows.

Unit 13 Cards and card readers

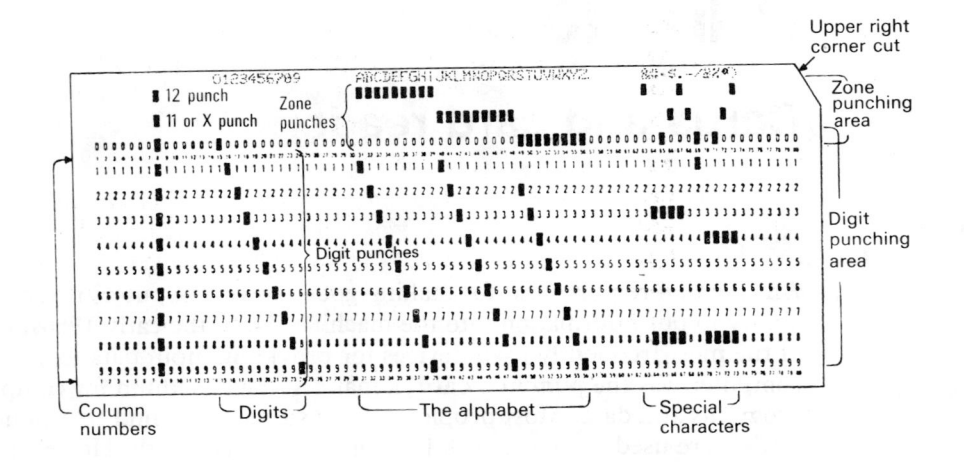

Figure 13.1 Punch Card

[4] Each of the digits, letters, and characters is represented by the particular pattern of punches in a column. Computer users can learn to read the patterns of the holes, but this is unnecessary since the characters can be printed at the top of the cards at the same time as the holes are punched. Because of this feature, both computer and user can easily read a punched card.

[5] Obviously, a card is ideal for storing binary information, with a hole representing 1, and no hole, 0. Information can be entered in this way, in which case the card is said to be a 'straight binary' card. But more often, information is entered in the Hollerith code or some other code. Then each column is read and interpreted individually, with a combination of punches in that column representing a specific character.

[6] Once the information has been converted into holes in the cards, it is ready for another piece of equipment called a card reader. This peripheral device is actually attached to the computer by a set of wires; hence, it is on-line. A stack of cards, or **deck**, is placed in the card reader face down. Cards are then examined one at a time within the reader by means of a light source with photosensitive elements which determine the presence or absence of a hole. This process is so fast that modern card readers can read up to 2,000 cards per minute. It should be noted that the card reader makes no use of the printed characters on the cards. These are there only to help the computer user interpret the cards, if necessary.

[7] In order to obtain still higher speeds, magnetic tape or disk is frequently used as an intermediate input medium. This is done by punching information on cards and then transferring it from cards to magnetic

Unit 13 Cards and card readers

tape or disk. The information can then be transmitted to the computer and stored in memory one word at a time by mounting the tape on a tape drive (or placing the disk on a disk drive) connected to the computer. This process is known as **spooling**.

[8] Recently, more and more programming is being done by keying-in the instructions at a display and keyboard unit rather than at a keypunch, and the same holds true for data entry. The programs and data then go directly to disk or magnetic tape, eliminating cards and card readers. However, no data processing installation today is without cards or card readers, because cards are frequently kept as a **backup system** in case of loss of data.

Exercises

1 Main idea

Which statement best express(es) the main idea of the text? Why did you eliminate the other choices?

☐ 1. Modern card readers are superior to their predecessors because of the speed at which they read cards.

☐ 2. Punched cards are going out of use.

☐ 3. Using punched cards is one way of storing information.

2 Understanding the passage

Decide whether the following statements are true or false (T/F) by referring to the information in the text. Then make the necessary changes so that the false statements become true.

T   F

☐ ☐ 1. Punched cards were invented by IBM to speed up the process of numerical analysis.

☐ ☐ 2. To transfer the information from the cards to memory, the card reader must be connected to the computer.

☐ ☐ 3. Punches on all computer cards are circular.

☐ ☐ 4. Every letter of the alphabet is represented by one hole on the card.

☐ ☐ 5. When the computer reads the holes, it translates the information to 0s or 1s.

☐ ☐ 6. The maximum number of characters that can be represented on any single card is 12, because each card has 12 rows.

Unit 13 Cards and card readers

T F

☐ ☐ 7. The characters that are punched on a card can be printed at the top so that the user can read them.

☐ ☐ 8. The keypunch and the card reader are considered peripheral devices.

☐ ☐ 9. The card reader reads the printed characters at the top of the card.

☐ ☐ 10. Terminals and display units have completely replaced the keypunch and the card reader.

3 Locating information

Find the passages in the text where the following ideas are expressed. Give the line references.

.... 1. The card reader must be on-line.
.... 2. The printed line at the top of the card is said to aid the user, not the computer.
.... 3. A card is a good way of storing binary information.
.... 4. Punched cards were used before 1960.
.... 5. Only 80 characters can be punched on one card.

4 Contextual reference

Look back at the text and find out what the words in **bold** typeface refer to.

1. **it** would take (*l. 10*) ....
2. The **first** is a keypunch (*l. 18*) ....
3. The **second** is a card reader (*l. 20*) ....
4. **which** is labelled (*l. 27*) ....
5. **which** is represented by (*l. 31*) ....
6. **it** is ready for (*l. 50*) ....
7. **which** determine the presence (*l. 55*) ....
8. **These** are only there to help (*l. 59*) ....
9. **This** is done by punching (*l. 62*) ....
10. then transferring **it** from cards (*l. 63*) ....

5 Understanding words

Refer back to the text and find synonyms for the following words.

1. thought up (*l. 12*) ....
2. identified (*l. 27*) ....
3. characteristic (*l. 41*) ....

Unit 13 Cards and card readers

4. transformed   (l. 50) ....
5. doing away with (l. 71) ....

Now refer back to the text and find antonyms for the following words.

6. minor   (l. 6) ....
7. slowing down   (l. 10) ....
8. punched   (l. 32) ....
9. essential   (l. 39) ....
10. absence   (l. 56) ....

6 Word forms

First choose the appropriate form of the words to complete the sentences. Then check the differences of meaning in your dictionary.

1. representation, represent, representative, represented, representing
   a. In the computer the letters of the alphabet are .... in terms of 0s and 1s.
   b. The Morse Code is composed of dots and dashes .... the letters of the alphabet and numerals.
   c. Each column of punched holes on a card .... a letter, a number, or a special character.
   d. The binary .... of the decimal number 10 is 1010.

2. recognition, recognize, recognized, recognizable
   a. It is easy to .... a JCL card because it usually precedes the program deck.
   b. Hollerith cards are .... by the cut right edge.

3. reference, refer, referred, referring, referrable
   a. The edge of the punched cards are cut off so as to give the user a .... point in placing the cards in the card reader.
   b. The person who punches cards is .... to as a keypunch operator.
   c. You should .... to the computer manual whenever you have a problem.

4. elimination, eliminate, eliminating, eliminator
   a. The programmer ran his program after .... all the bugs from it.
   b. Storing programs and data on disks and magnetic tapes has resulted in the .... of cards and card readers.
   c. My supervisor asked me to .... all the unnecessary details from the program documentation.

5. interpretation, interpret, interpreted, interpreter
   a. Each column of the punched card is read and .... individually with a combination of holes in that column representing a specific character.
   b. For the .... of IBM assembly language you should be familiar with the hexadecimal number system.
   c. The printed characters on a card are there only to help the computer user .... the card if necessary.

7 Content review

Match the following words in column A with the corresponding information in column B.

A
1. off-line
2. punched card
3. card reader
4. zone punch row
5. on-line
6. deck
7. spooling
8. keypunch operator
9. keypunch
10. backup system

B
a. a set of cards
b. a kind of typewriter
c. transfer information from cards to tape or disk
d. not linked to memory
e. used if data is lost
f. should be on-line
g. storage medium
h. connected to the computer
i. found at the top of the card
j. a computer typist

8 Focus review

Focus G   Time sequence

First complete the following table by referring back to the text on 'Cards and Card Readers'.

TIME SEQUENCE MARKER	INFORMATION
1.	Punched cards were used on textile machinery
2.	The first application of punched cards for the representation of large amounts of data

Unit 13 Cards and card readers

TIME SEQUENCE MARKER	INFORMATION
3.	IBM was founded which produced the necessary machines to meet Dr. Hollerith's needs
4.	Punched cards were one of the most frequently used devices for providing input data

Now re-order the following information so that the events appear in the correct sequence. (Number the events 1–5.) Refer back to paragraphs 5 and 6 of 'Cards and Card Readers'.

☐ a. Once the information has been punched on the cards, they are ready to be read.

☐ b. Only after this has been done will the information be read by a photosensitive light, one column at a time.

☐ c. Information is usually entered on cards in the Hollerith code or some other code.

☐ d. Modern card readers can read up to 2,000 cards per minute.

☐ e. The cards are then stacked and put face down in the card reader.

Focus J   Giving an explanation or definition

In the following sentences, which were taken from the text on 'Cards and Card Readers', underline the part of the sentence which gives an explanation or a definition, then circle the term which is being explained or defined.

Example

Until the early 1960s, one of the most frequently used devices for providing input data to computer was the (punched card,) a major storage medium for computer programs and data.

1. Dr. Hollerith went on to found a company to produce these machines, which in 1924 became International Business Machines, or IBM for short.
2. The keypunch, which looks like a large typewriter, is not physically connected to the computer.
3. Obviously, a card is ideal for storing binary information, with a hole representing 1, and a no hole, 0.
4. The card reader is actually attached to the computer by a set of wires; hence it is on-line.

FOCUS K

Classifying

The term 'classification' means to separate objects from one another. The simplest classification divides things into those that show groups of characteristics that are shared and those that are not. For example, one would not place fish and birds together in the same class with trees. Classification usually goes from general to specific and is essential in attempting to make sense out of things around us.

Classification, then, is a process of bringing order out of confusion by breaking down the general topic into its related parts in a logical way. Outlining is very closely related to classification, because it organizes information in a logical fashion, going from general to specific, or from least important to most important, or from specific to general.

1 From general to specific

There are several ways of expressing each of these relationships. By focusing on the large or high-level category and talking about its parts, that is, *from general to specific*, the following expressions can be used:

is	is made up of
can be divided into	is composed of
is of	comprises
has	consists of
includes	

A general to specific classification will usually have singular main verbs, unless two or more things are being analysed simultaneously.

Examples
1. The CPU **is divided into** three parts: the control unit, the arithmetic-logical unit, and memory.
2. The CPU **has** three parts: the control unit, the arithmetic-logical unit, and memory.
3. The CPU **includes** three parts: the control unit, the arithmetic-logical unit, and memory.

4. The CPU **is made up of** three parts: the control unit, the arithmetic-logical unit, and memory.
5. The CPU **is composed of** three parts: the control unit, the arithmetic-logical unit, and memory.
6. The CPU **consists of** three parts: the control unit, the arithmetic-logical unit, and memory.

2   From specific to general

A *specific to general classification*, what the smaller (or lower-level) components make when they are put together, usually has the following expressions:

are ... of	constitute
make up	may be
form	can be
	are classified as

A specific to general classification will have plural verbs, because two or more lower-level categories are the focus of classification.

Examples

1. The control unit, the arithmetic-logical unit, and memory **are** the three parts **of** the CPU.
2. The control unit, the arithmetic-logical unit, and memory are the three parts that **make up** the CPU.
3. The control unit, the arithmetic-logical unit, and memory are the three parts that **form** the CPU.
4. The control unit, the arithmetic-logical unit and memory are the three parts that **constitute** the CPU.
5. The control unit, the arithmetic-logical unit, and memory together **are classified as** the CPU.

N.B. The active/passive pairs such as **made up** and **make up** are *not* interchangeable.

Example

The CPU is **made up of** the control unit, the arithmetic-logical unit, and memory. *(from general to specific.)*

Not: 'The CPU **makes up** the control unit, the arithmetic-logical unit, and memory.'

Not: 'The control unit, the arithmetic-logical unit, and memory **are made up of** the CPU.'

Finally, understanding classification is important for understanding and recognizing definitions.

Exercise 1

Refer back to Units 9 and 10 and while reading complete the diagram.

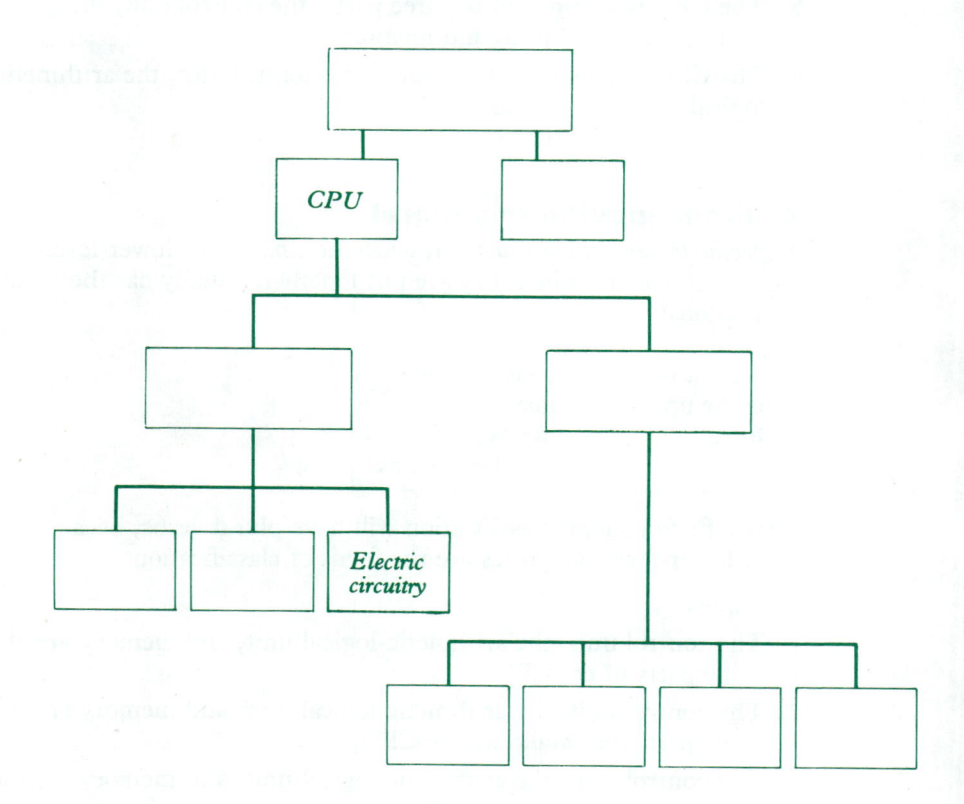

CPU

Electric circuitry

Focus K Classifying

Exercise 2
Using the diagram below, complete the paragraph that follows.

A Computer system

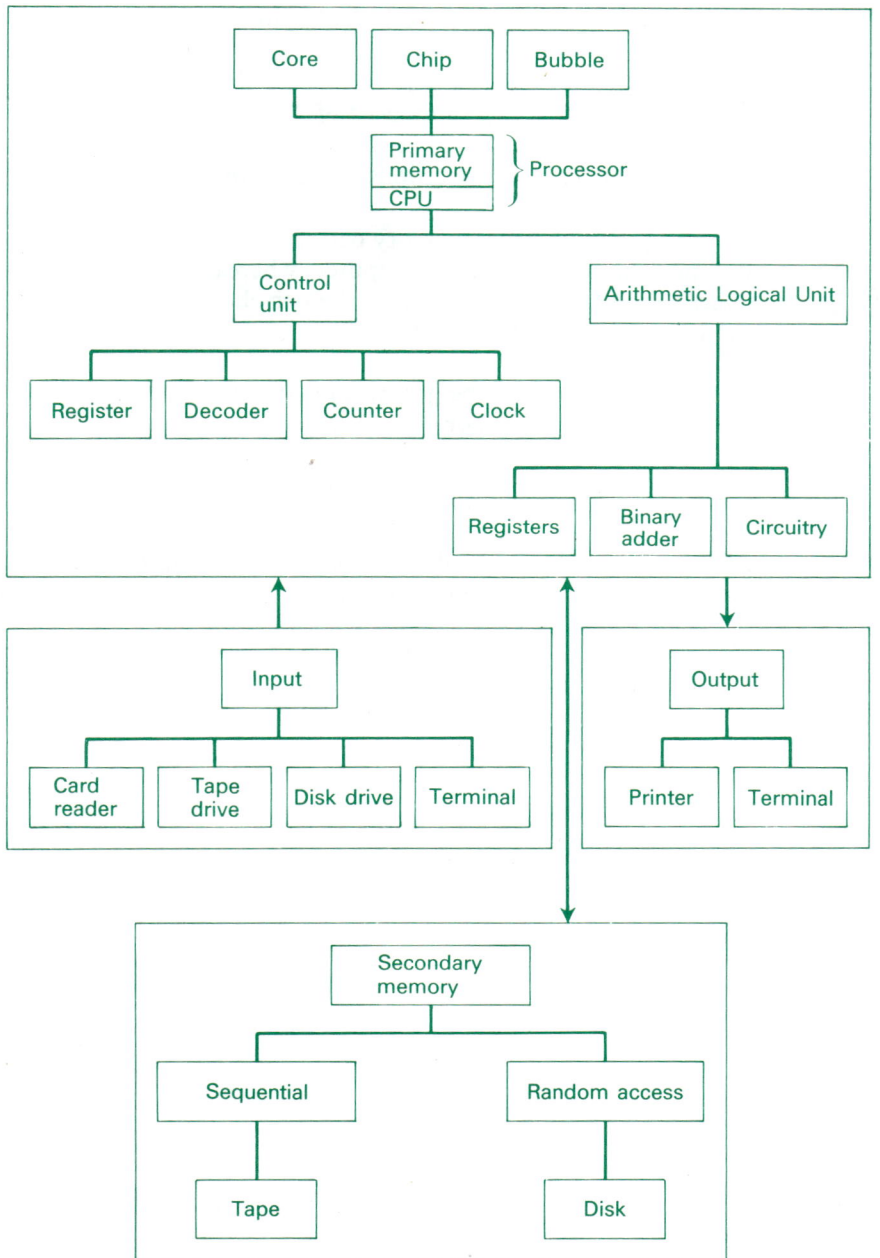

A computer has four basic components: input, processor, memory, and output. The CPU consists of two parts: the .... which directs and controls the signals and commands inside the processor, and the .... unit which does the arithmetic operations and the decision-making operations. While the .... is made up of a ...., a ...., a .... and a ...., the .... is composed of ...., a .... and ...., which compares information and makes decisions based on the results of the comparisons.

In a computer, internal memory or .... refers to the storage locations inside the computer, whereas .... refers to the storage embodied in the peripherals. .... can be divided into three types: ...., ... and .... on the other hand may be grouped as .... (.................................) or .... (.................................).

The .... devices can be either a ...., a ...., a .... or a ....

These devices enter the information into the computer. After the processor has operated on it, the .... devices display the results of the computations on either a .... or a ...., or store them on tape or disk for future use.

UNIT 14

Tapes and tape drives

[1] There are two kinds of secondary memory technologies: sequential and random-access or direct-access. An example of the former is a strip of plastic, usually half an inch wide, coated on one side with metal oxide that can be magnetized. Tapes come in varying lengths of 250, 600, 1200, and 2400 feet and are usually kept off-line in libraries. When the information stored on tape is needed, an operator mounts the tape onto a tape drive which has a fixed **reel** and an empty **hub**. The tape is then threaded through the machine in a way similar to that of threading a tape through a tape recorder.

[2] To mark the beginning and the end of a tape, small pieces of silver foil or any other reflective strips called **tape-marks** are stuck onto the tape. Information is then stored on the tape in magnetized units called **bits** which are similar to the bits in internal memory. Vertically, they form patterns such that every nine of them (eight bits of data plus a **parity** bit, used for error detection) are called a **frame**. A group of these frames forms a **record** of information, which may be either long or short. These records are separated from each other by marks called interrecord gaps, and a group of such logical records forms a physical record known as a **block**. Blocks, in turn, are organized as **files**, which are separated from each other by special characters.

[3] How much information is stored on the tape depends on the length of the tape as well as its **density**. The density is determined by the number of bytes that can be stored on one inch of tape and is measured by **bytes per inch** or BPI. Some tapes store information at a density of 1600 BPI or even 6250 BPI, which means that at the latter density, 2400 feet of tape would be needed to store approximately 175 million bytes of information.

[4] Tape drives record information lengthwise in **channels** or **tracks**, with one bit per track. Newer models use nine tracks rather than seven as the older models did. In order to store information on a tape, a tape drive is equipped with a set of recording heads, one head per track. One tape drive is distinguished from another by the **transfer rate** or **transfer speed**; in other words, by the number of bytes per second a tape drive is capable of transferring from the tape to the memory or vice versa. This

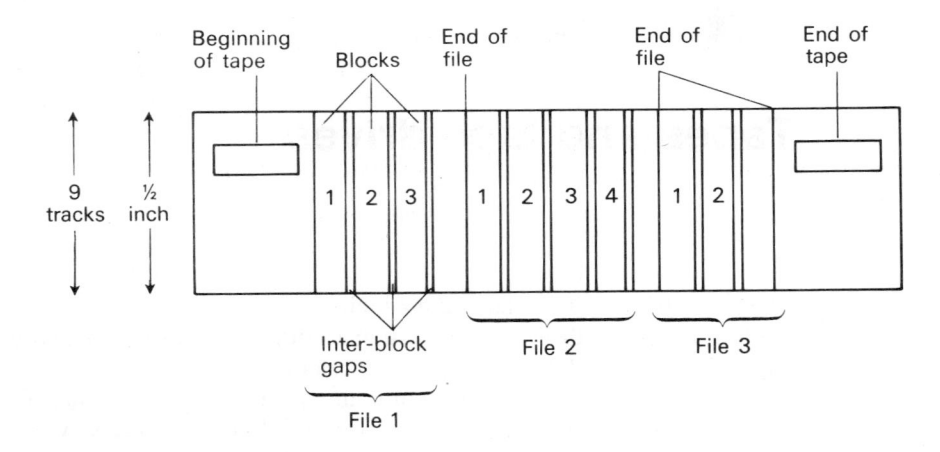

Figure 14.1 Section of magnetic tape

speed is usually measured by inches per second, or IPS. So, if a tape drive has a transfer speed of 200 IPS, reading from a 6250 BPI density tape is like reading about 15,000 cards in one second!

[5] Tapes are obviously a faster medium than punched cards for accessing information; moreover, they require less space in the library. Because they can be mailed, they are a convenient way to transfer data from one computer to another, or even from one city to another.

Exercises

1 Main idea

Which statement best expresses the main idea of the text? Why did you eliminate the other choices?

☐ 1. Tapes are organized in terms of frames, records, blocks, and files.

☐ 2. Tapes differ from each other by the transfer rate they have.

☐ 3. It is easy to transfer information from one computer to another by means of tapes.

2 Understanding the passage

Decide whether the following statements are true or false (T/F) by referring to the information in the text. Then make the necessary changes so that the false statements become true.

T F
☐ ☐ 1. The magnetic tape is an example of a random-access device.
☐ ☐ 2. Tapes are usually kept on-line.
☐ ☐ 3. To read a tape, you put it on the hub of a tape drive.
☐ ☐ 4. All tapes have nine tracks.
☐ ☐ 5. Information is stored lengthwise on a tape.
☐ ☐ 6. The amount of information stored on a tape depends on the density and the length of the tape.
☐ ☐ 7. Transfer speed refers to the number of words a tape can transfer from one tape to another.
☐ ☐ 8. Tapes are superior to cards, partly because they require less space for storage.
☐ ☐ 9. A group of frames constitutes a block.
☐ ☐ 10. Blocks are separated from one another by reflective strips which are stuck on the tape.

3 Locating information

Find the passages in the text where the following ideas are expressed. Give the line references.

.... 1. Tapes are characterized by the rate they transfer information to the memory.
.... 2. A record varies in length.
.... 3. To get information from a tape, the operator puts it onto the tape drive.
.... 4. Tapes are faster than punched cards.
.... 5. How much information a tape has depends on two things.

4 Contextual reference

Look back at the text and find out what the words in **bold** typeface refer to.

1. An example of the **former** is   (l. 2) ....
2. **which** has a fixed reel   (l. 7) ....
3. similar to **that** of threading   (l. 8) ....

4. **which** are similar to the bits (l. 13) ....
5. vertically **they** form patterns (l. 13) ....
6. a group of **such** logical (l. 18) ....
7. **which** are separated from (l. 19) ....
8. as well as **its** density (l. 22) ....
9. that at the **latter** density (l. 25) ....
10. **they** require less space (l. 39) ....

5 Understanding words

Refer back to the text and find synonyms for the following words.

1. differentiated (l. 32) ....
2. the other way around (l. 34) ....
3. need (l. 39) ....
4. handy (l. 40) ....
5. move information (l. 40) ....

Now refer back to the text and find antonyms for the following words.

6. primary (l. 1) ....
7. fixed (l. 4) ....
8. horizontally (l. 13) ....
9. subdivided into (l. 19) ....
10. connected to (l. 19) ....

6 Word forms

First choose the appropriate form of the words to complete the sentences. Then check the differences of meaning in your dictionary.

1. reflection, reflect, reflective, reflector
   a. The surface of this plastic tape .... light, giving it a silvery color.
   b. .... plastic pieces are stuck onto the tape to mark its beginning.

2. storage, store, stored, storing
   a. The computer memory is capable of .... a lot of information for a short period of time.
   b. The recording heads of a tape drive access the information which is .... on a tape.
   c. There are now telephones that can .... up to fifteen numbers in their memory.

3. transfer, transference, transferred, transferable
   a. To .... information from a tape to the memory, the tape is mounted on a tape drive.
   b. Tape drives differ from each other by the .... rate they have.
   c. The results of calculations are .... to memory from the ALU.

4. capability, capable, capably
   a. A computer is .... of performing repetitive operations at a very fast rate.
   b. Until the .... and limitations of a computer are recognized, its usefulness cannot be thoroughly understood.

5. organization, organize, organized, organizing, organizer
   a. Blocks are .... in terms of files.
   b. The efficiency of a computer centre depends partly on its .... and personnel.
   c. The computer centre is planning to .... guided tours of the computer room.

7 Content review

Write the appropriate word(s) for the following definitions.

.... 1. circular plastic around which the tape is threaded

.... 2. a group of blocks

.... 3. central piece of plastic around which a reel fits

.... 4. a group of frames

.... 5. number of bytes per inch on a tape

.... 6. channel to record data on tape

.... 7. a group of records

.... 8. small pieces to mark the beginning or the end of a tape

.... 9. vertical pattern of bits on a tape

.... 10. a bit to detect errors

8 Focus review

Focus F Making comparisons

First look at the following sentences from Unit 14, 'Tapes and Tape Drives'. Decide whether the sentences express: a. equivalence; b. non-equivalence; or c. the superlative, then underline the words expressing the comparison.

....	1. The tape is then threaded through the machine in a way similar to that of threading a tape through a tape recorder.
....	2. How much information is stored on the tape depends on the length of the tape as well as its density.
....	3. Newer models use nine tracks rather than seven as the older models did.
....	4. If a tape drive has a transfer speed of 200 IPS, reading from a 6250 BPI density tape is like reading about 15,000 cards in one second.
....	5. Tapes are obviously a faster medium than punched cards for accessing information.
....	6. Moreover, tapes require *less* space in the library.

Now read the text on 'Cards and Card Readers' again, and as you read, complete the table below by writing the sentence or that part of the sentence that expresses a comparison.

PARA	EQUIVALENCE	NON-EQUIVALENCE	SUPERLATIVE
[1]			
[2]			
[3]			
[4]	at the same time as the holes are punched		

Focus K Classifying

Read paragraph 2 of 'Tapes and Tape Drives' again, then label the following diagram.

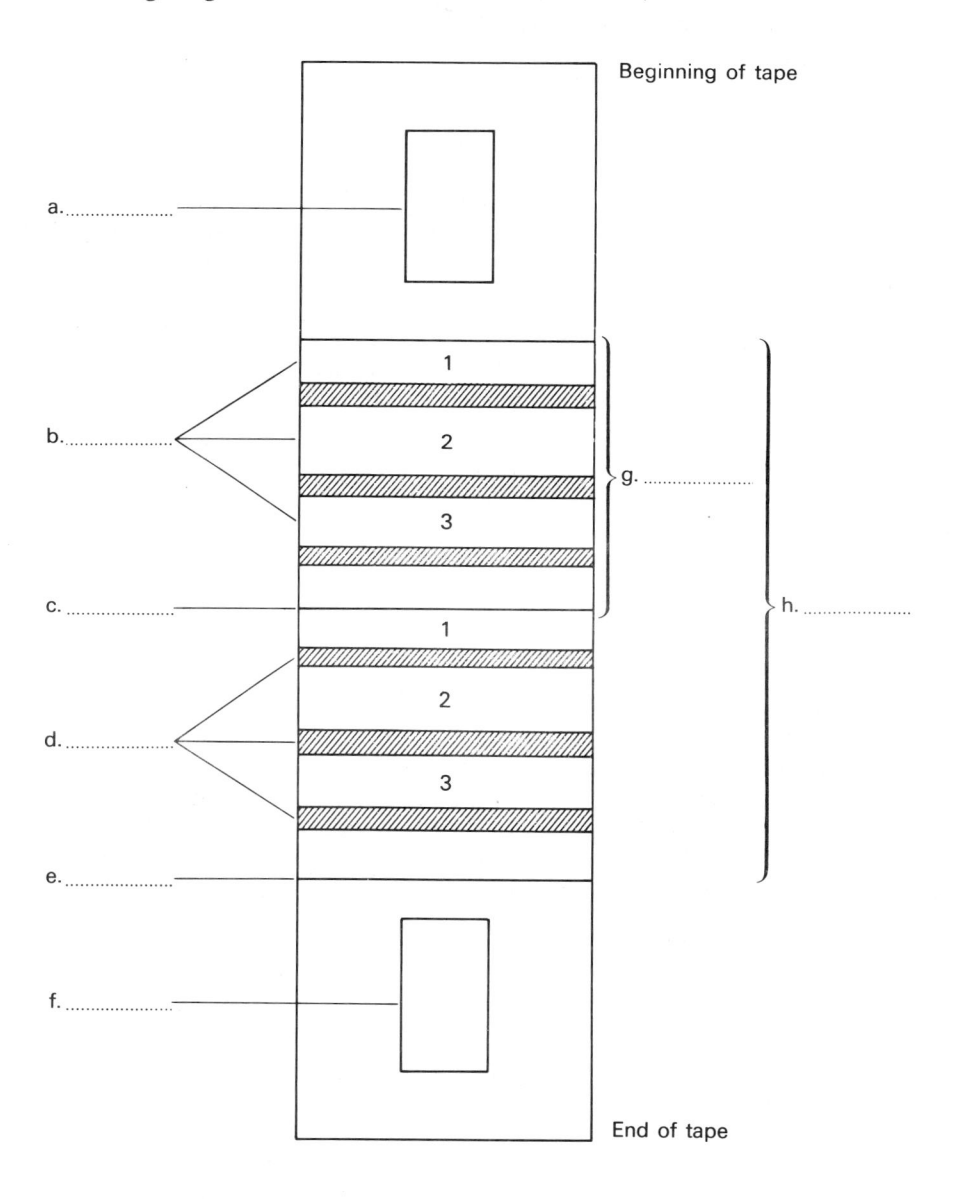

Beginning of tape

a. ....
b. ....
c. ....
d. ....
e. ....
f. ....
g. ....
h. ....

End of tape

UNIT 15

Disks and disk drives

[1] Tapes are an example of sequential-access memory technology; an example of random-access or direct-access secondary memory devices is the magnetic disk. It provides a large amount of storage and rapid retrieval of any stored information. All disks are made of a substance coated with metal oxide, and can therefore be magnetized.

[2] Magnetic disks are of two kinds, namely **floppy** and **hard**. The hard disks, in turn, are subdivided into **fixed-head** and **moving-head** disks which are either **cartridge** or **pack**. Floppy disks, or **diskettes** as they are called, are made from plastic, which makes them very light, flexible, and quite inexpensive, whereas hard disks are made from a rigid material.

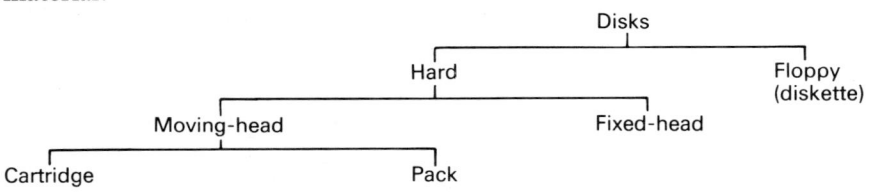

```
                              Disks
                 ┌──────────────┴──────────────┐
                Hard                     Floppy (diskette)
      ┌──────────┴──────────┐
  Moving-head           Fixed-head
  ┌────┴────┐
Cartridge  Pack
```

A disk cartridge is made of a circular disk called a **platter**, about the same size as a long-playing record, which can be magnetized on both sides. When a number of these circular platters are stacked one on top of the other, they are called a disk pack. How many platters there are in a disk pack varies depending on the manufacturer and the model.

[3] The recording surface of a disk has concentric circles called **tracks**,

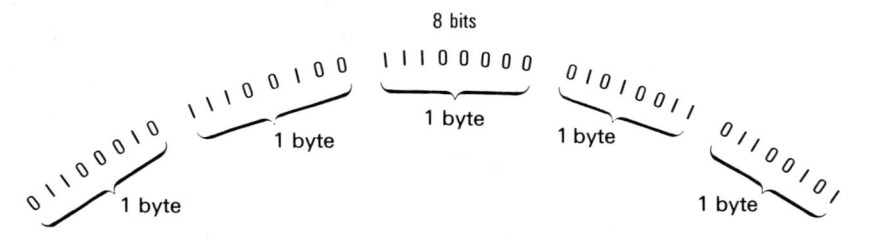

Figure 15.1 Part of a track

which are similar to the grooves in a record. Information is stored on a track in magnetized spots called bits. These bits are similar to the bits in internal memory and are situated on the track such that usually every eight of them make up one byte.

[4] To access information from a cartridge, it is mounted on a disk drive which is equipped with two **recording heads**, one for each side of the disk. The heads move radially along a line from the center to the outside from track to track. To access information from a disk pack, the recording heads are moved back and forth in the space between the platters by the access arms to which they are attached.

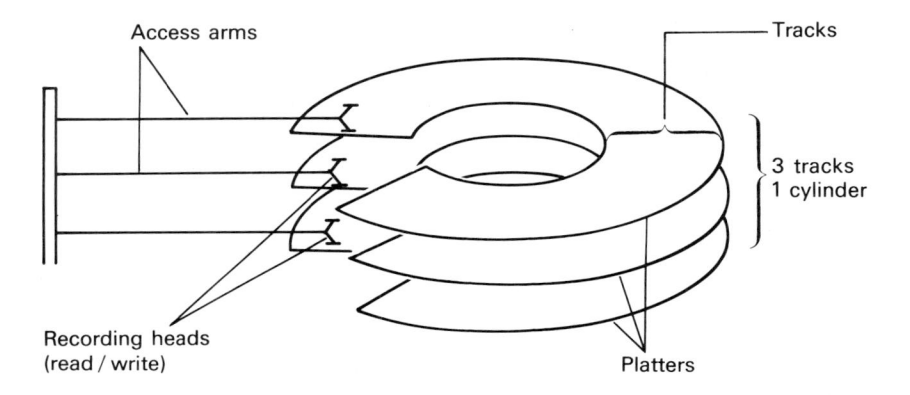

Figure 15.2 Disk pack

A stack of tracks is called a **cylinder** and it is accessed by all the recording heads acting at once. The recording capacity of a disk pack is measured in terms of a number of cylinders, the number of tracks, and the amount of data in each track.

[5] Information on a disk is organized in terms of blocks, each having its own address, which consists of a cylinder number, a track number, and a record number. To access directly the necessary information, the recording heads first seek the required cylinder, then search to find the beginning of the required record, and then transfer the information to the memory of the computer or to another form of storage, all of which is done in a few milliseconds.

[6] Dust and dirt cause the recording condition of disks to deteriorate. As a result, **data packs**, which are disks with the recording heads sealed inside, were developed. They are more expensive than the normal disk packs but the drives on which they are mounted are cheaper than the normal disk drives.

[7] Disk drives are of two kinds: drives with a single non-removable platter, and drives in which disks can be changed. The latter kind is further subdivided into top-loading single platter, front-loading single platter, and top-loading multiple platter. Some disk drives open from the top, where single platter disks are placed. Other drives open in the front and single platter disks, either hard disks or diskettes, are inserted. For very long storage, the top-loading multiple platter drives are used. After being mounted on a disk drive, disks are kept spinning at a very high and constant speed, thus allowing the recording heads to have direct access to the required information. For example, the pack on the IBM 3330 spins at 60 revolutions per second.

Exercises

1 Main idea
Which statement best expresses the main idea of the text? Why did you eliminate the other choices?

☐ 1. There are many different types of magnetic disks and disk drives.

☐ 2. It takes a very short time to access information from disks.

☐ 3. Disks provide more storage than tapes, and therefore are more expensive.

2 Understanding the passage
Decide whether the following statements are true or false (T/F) by referring to the information in the text. Then make the necessary changes so that the false statements become true.

T F
☐ ☐ 1. Magnetic disks are better than magnetic tapes only because they provide large amounts of storage.

☐ ☐ 2. Disk packs are fixed-head disks.

☐ ☐ 3. Not all disks are made from a rigid material.

☐ ☐ 4. There are two platters in each disk carriage.

☐ ☐ 5. The number of platters in a disk depends on the company that makes it.

☐ ☐ 6. Bits are magnetized grooves in the surface of a disk.

☐ ☐ 7. To access information, the recording heads move from one groove to another.

Unit 15 Disks and disk drives

T F
☐ ☐ 8. Information on cylinders is accessed one track at a time.
☐ ☐ 9. The recording heads in a data pack are part of the disk and not the disk drive.
☐ ☐ 10. There are three kinds of disk drives.

3 Locating information
Find the passages in the text where the following ideas are expressed. Give the line references.

.... 1. Recording heads read from both sides of a cartridge.
.... 2. When disks are put on disk drives, they start spinning.
.... 3. Disk packs have more than one platter.
.... 4. The number of platters in a disk depends on the manufacturer.
.... 5. Recording heads are capable of transferring information from a disk to the memory of the computer.

4 Contextual reference
Look back at the text and find out what the words in **bold** typeface refer to.

1. **It** provides a large amount   (l. 3)   ....
2. disks **which** are either   (l. 8)   ....
3. **which** makes them   (l. 9)   ....
4. **which** can be magnetized   (l. 13)   ....
5. **it** is mounted on a disk drive   (l. 22)   ....
6. to which **they** are attached   (l. 27)   ....
7. having **its** own address   (l. 32)   ....
8. **all of which** is done   (l. 37)   ....
9. on which **they** are mounted   (l. 42)   ....
10. the **latter** kind is further subdivided (l. 45) ....

5 Understanding words
Refer back to the text and find synonyms for the following words.

1. fast   (l. 3)   ....
2. finding   (l. 4)   ....
3. piled up   (l. 14)   ....
4. look for   (l. 35)   ....
5. become worse   (l. 39)   ....

Now refer back to the text and find antonyms for the following words.

6. rigid (l. 9) ....
7. unmagnetized (l. 13) ....
8. dissimilar (l. 18) ....
9. external (l. 20) ....
10. single (l. 47) ....

6 Word forms

First choose the appropriate form of the words to complete the sentences. Then check the differences of meaning in your dictionary.

1. magnet, magnetism, magnetic, magnetize, magnetized, magnetization, magnetizing
   a. Both tapes and disks are considered .... storage media.
   b. Information is recorded on a disk in the form of .... spots called bits.
   c. .... is the principle underlying the storage of information in computer memories.

2. record, recorder, recording, recorded
   a. Disk drives have two sets of .... heads which move from track to track to access information.
   b. Information .... on disks can be accessed much faster than information .... on tapes.
   c. Computers are capable of storing a lot of information by .... it on tapes or disks.

3. access, accessible, accessibility, accessed, accessing
   a. Do you have .... to the student files in the database?
   b. To .... information recorded on a disk, a disk drive must be used.
   c. Tapes are a faster medium than punched cards for .... information.
   d. A cylinder is .... by all the recording heads acting at once.

4. requirement, require, requiring, required
   a. One of the .... of a good computer programmer is to have a logical mind.
   b. Our university .... foreign students to take a proficiency exam in the English language before registering for a computer science degree.

Unit 15 Disks and disk drives

c. Students wishing to major in computer science are .... to know how the computer operates.

5. measurement, measure, measured, measuring, measurable
   a. The analog computer is used essentially for problems involving ....
   b. The density of a tape is .... by bytes per inch.
   c. The number of bytes per second a tape drive is capable of transferring from a tape to the memory of the computer must be considered in .... the transfer speed.
   d. To .... the recording capacity of a disk, you must consider the number of cylinders, the number of tracks, and the amount of data in each track.

7a Content review

Try to think of a definition for each of these items before checking them in the Glossary. Then complete the following statements with the appropriate words. (Some can be used more than once.) Make sure you use the correct form, i.e. singular or plural.

cylinder	hard disk	fixed-head
platters	pack	recording head
cartridge	diskette	moving-head
data pack		

1. Floppy disks which are made from plastic are also called ....
2. A .... is accessed by all the recording heads acting at once.
3. Disks which are not made from flexible plastic are called ....
4. When more than one platter are piled on top of each other it is referred to as a ....
5. The .... access information from either side of a disk.
6. .... can be either single or multiple.
7. A .... has a single platter.
8/9. Hard disks can be subdivided into two kinds: .... and ....
10. When the recording heads are included with the platters, it is called a ....

7b Content review

Complete the following diagram by adding the relevant information associated with each type of disk.

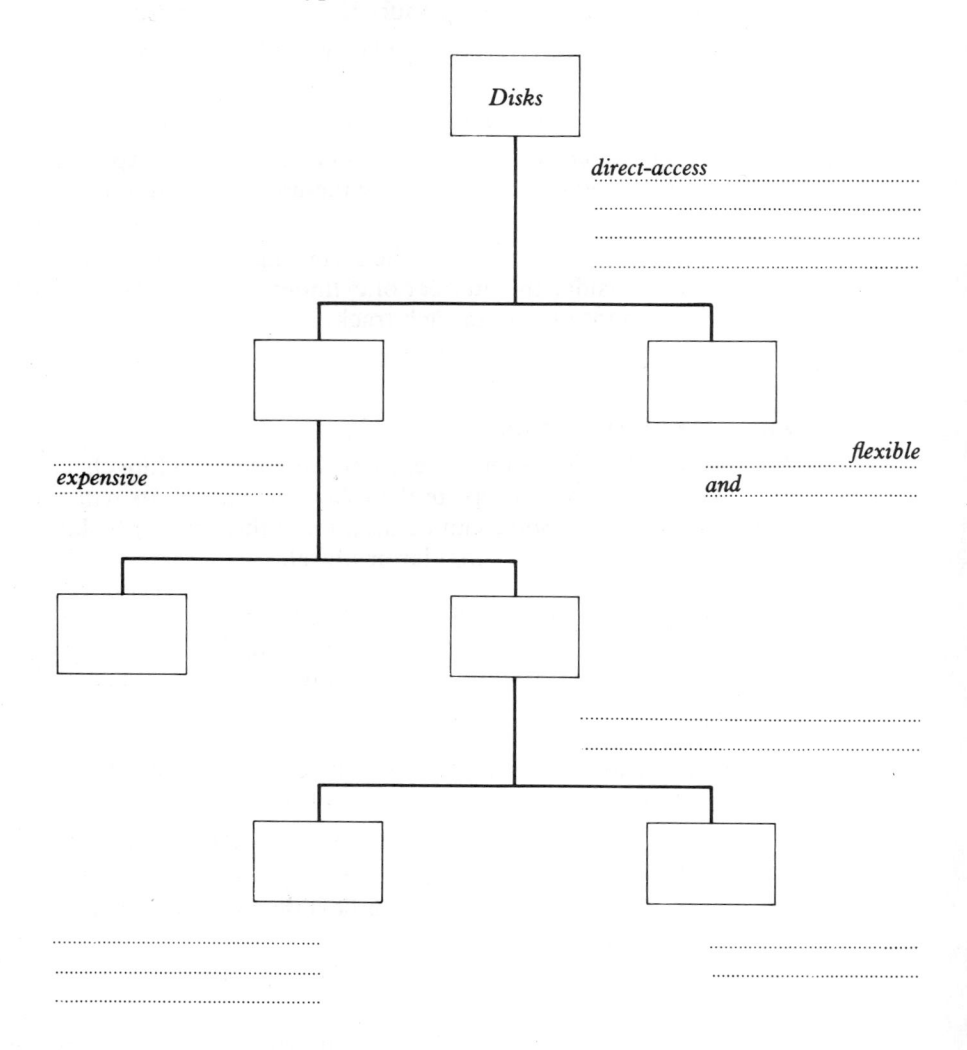

direct-access

expensive

flexible
and

7c Content review

Summarize the information in Units 13, 14, and 15 by completing the following table.

	CARDS	TAPES	DISKS
Material	paper		1. floppy 2. hard
Equipment needed		tape drive	
How information is stored	each card has 12 vertical rows which can be punched representing (0s) or left unpunched (1s)		
How much information is stored			depends on the number of platters in a disk and the density of the disk
How information is organized			bits on a track; tracks divided into sectors: groups of sectors – a record; groups or records
How information is transferred		tape drives with recording heads read from or write on tapes	
Type of access	sequential, a card at a time		
Speed of access	depends on rate a card reader reads per minute		
Reason for use nowadays	backup system in computer installations		
Cost			

8 Focus review

Focus G   Time sequence

Re-read paragraph 5 of 'Disks and Disks Drives' and complete the table below on the functions of the recording heads of a disk drive.

SEQUENCE MARKER	EVENT
	SEEK the required cylinder

Focus K   Classifying

Re-read paragraph 6 of 'Disks and Disk Drives' and, while reading, complete the following diagram

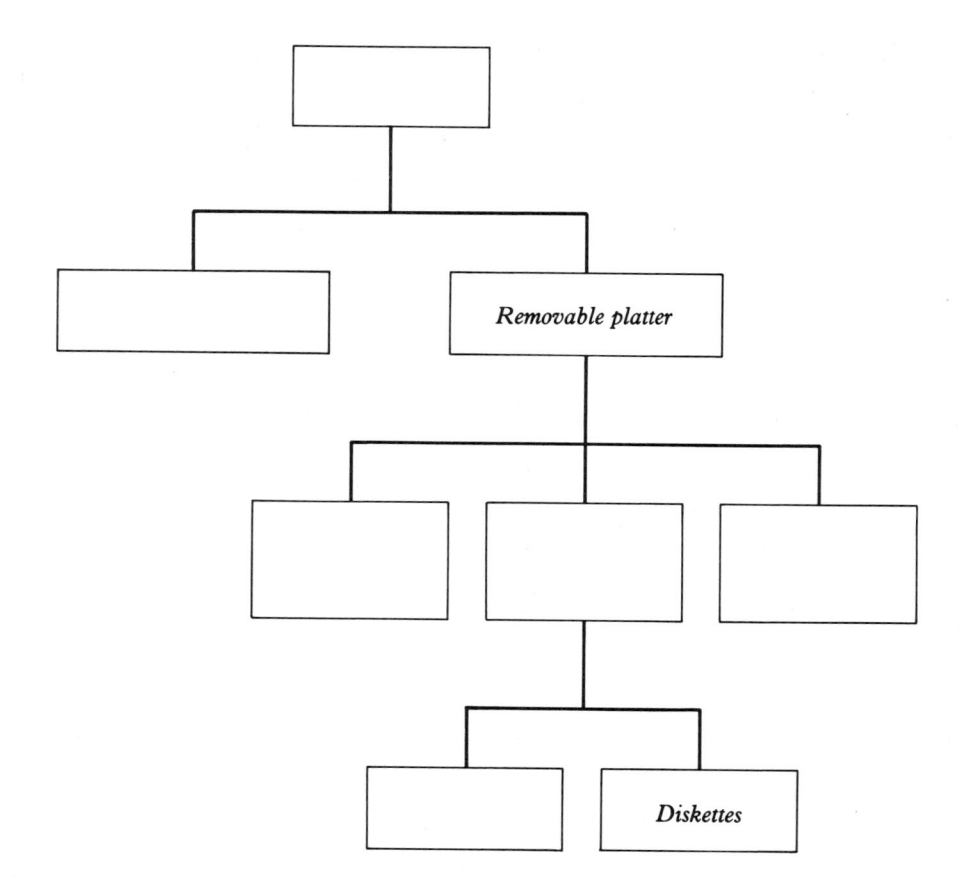

```
            ┌─────────┐
            │         │
            └────┬────┘
         ┌───────┴───────┐
    ┌────┴─────┐   ┌─────┴────────────┐
    │          │   │ Removable platter │
    └──────────┘   └─────┬────────────┘
                 ┌───────┼───────┐
            ┌────┴──┐ ┌──┴──┐ ┌──┴────┐
            │       │ │     │ │       │
            └───────┘ └──┬──┘ └───────┘
                    ┌────┴────┬──────────┐
                    │         │ Diskettes│
                    └─────────┘└─────────┘
```

FOCUS L

Contrasting

Reading texts often have connectives omitted without seriously affecting the flow of intelligibility. However, connectives dealing with contrastive elements within a sentence or paragraph are very rarely absent because without these, the reading passage would be nonsensical and confusing. There are many ways of showing that contrast exists between things.

1 The easiest indicator that *a contrast* exists and that also emphasizes that the *opposite* is true, is when a statement is introduced by one of the following markers:

on the contrary	conversely
on the one hand; ... on the other hand	opposite
	in comparison
by contrast	by way of contrast

Examples
1. The control unit transmits coordinating control signals and commands; **on the other hand**, the arithmetic-logical unit performs the arithmetic and logical operations called for in the instruction.
2. Magnetic tapes are cheap, but access to specified data may take time **in comparison** with disks, which are expensive and permit direct or almost direct-access to specified data.
3. A computer can solve a complex problem in seconds; **by way of contrast**, man would take weeks, maybe months, to do the same operations.

2 Sometimes contrastive connectives are used to indicate that what follows is a *replacement* of what was said before. Examples of such markers are:

alternatively	rather
instead	an/the alternative is ...*
but	It might be better if ...*
then	whereas
*occurs in initial position	

Examples
1. Second-generation computers worked faster than their predecessors because of the use of transistors **instead** of vacuum tubes.
2. When a computer fails to produce the desired output, it is often due to human error **rather than** the fault of the computer itself.
3. A 'smaller' computer may take several steps to perform some given operation, **whereas** a 'larger' machine may accomplish the same thing with one instruction.

3 When the writer wants to express that what has been said before is true or correct, but what follows is, *in contrast*, also true or correct, the following connective markers are used:

but	in spite of
however	despite that
nevertheless	on the other hand
nonetheless	even if
although	even though
though	

Examples
1. Computers have a means of communicating with the user. **However**, certain computers (commonly minicomputers and microcomputers) are used to control directly things such as robots and aircraft navigation systems.
2. A computer can replace people in dull, routine tasks, **but** it has no originality.
3. Computers have often been thought of as very large adding machines. **Although** a computer can only respond to a certain number of instructions, it is not a single-purpose machine.

Exercise 1

Read again 'Cards and Card Readers' (Unit 13) and while reading complete the table below.

PARA	CONTRASTIVE MARKERS	ITEMS CONTRASTED
[1]	*however*	
[3]		*types of punches*
[5]	*but*	
[8]		*input devices*

Focus L Contrasting

Exercise 2

Complete the table below by referring back to the appropriate units and paragraphs as indicated in the first column of the table.

UNIT [PARA]	CONTRASTIVE MARKER	FUNCTION OF MARKER	ITEMS CONTRASTED
1 [3]	however		
1 [5]			originality
2 [5]		replacement	
3 [4]	although		
4 [3]			time
4 [4]		opposite and true	
4 [4]	however		
6 [1]			operation
7 [1]		contrast and true	
7 [1]	however		
8 [1]			memory
8 [4]		contrast and true	
9 [5]	on the other hand		
11 [3]			use
11 [4]		opposite	
12 [2]	whereas		

UNIT 16

Printers

[1] Printed output, which can be read by humans rather than by a computer, is the most common output. It is two-dimensional, consisting of characters within a line, and lines on a page. One of the most difficult parts of printing output is the reaction of the user to the printed page, because somehow the printed output produces a response from the reader much like that of people to a roomful of new furniture. They have definite ideas where each piece should go, but after seeing it there, they are apt to change their minds. The same occurs when the reader first sees the printed output of a report, for instance.

[2] No matter how simple or complex the data-processing operation is, the final results must be made available in a form usable by humans, and usually in the form of a permanent record. This is the purpose of the printers used with computing equipment.

[3] Printers vary in speed, size, and cost, and are designed to meet printing requirements ranging from roughly the speed and volume of a typewriter up to thousands of lines per minute. There are two ways of printing: by **impact** (striking a character through a carbon, like a typewriter) or **non-impact** (photocopying, like an office copier). Impact printers are generally a **drum**, or a **chain** or **train**. The drum has a spinning cylinder for each character position in a line, and each cylinder contains all the characters in a character set. As each cylinder spins into the appropriate character position, it is hammered onto the paper through a carbon ribbon. Drum printers generally give the lowest quality printing, because if the hammer hits a little early or late, the character will appear slightly above or below the line. This is noticeable on a printed line, giving it a wavy appearance.

[4] In train or chain printers, the characters move laterally across the page, and as the proper character moves into position, it is hammered onto the paper through a carbon ribbon. If the hammer hits a little early or late, the character will appear slightly to the right or left of its proper position, but variations in horizontal spacing are not so noticeable to humans.

[5] Other types of impact printers are the **daisy wheel printer**, the **matrix printer**, and the **line printer**. The daisy wheel printer uses a wheel with up to 100 characters, each being on an individual arm, so that only

rotation is needed. The hammer hits a single letter, guaranteeing accurate positioning and uniform striking. This allows a fast, quiet, and reliable operation, with superb print quality.

[6] A matrix printer, on the other hand, uses pins to print a pattern of dots on paper. The characters are generated by selecting the appropriate combinations of pins in a rectangle of 5 rows by 7 columns or 9 columns. Each pin is equipped with a coil, which, when energized, throws the pin against the ribbon, printing a dot on the paper. For each character, seven or nine lines of dots have to be printed; however, the inertia is minimal, so fast operation is possible. The general advantages of using matrix printers are relative low cost, high speed, and quiet operation. The main disadvantage is the relatively poor quality of printing, which is sufficiently good for the eye, but not for reproduction or for business letters.

[7] Finally, the printing mechanism in line printers is completely different from matrix printers. In the line printer, the character set to be printed is on a cylinder where each segment has the full set of characters in raised form around its edge. All segments are aligned with one another; that is, all the 'As', for example, are in line. Whenever the printer is in print mode, the cylinder is rotating and each character in the set passes by the line to be printed as one complete revolution of the cylinder is made. The printer times the movement of a print hammer so that the character on the cylinder segment is brought into contact with the ribbon and paper. One complete line of characters is printed during one revolution of the cylinder. It is interesting to note that all the 'As' used in the line are printed first, then all the 'Bs', and so on until finally all the letters that make up the words have been printed and the line is complete. Whereas 200 to 600 lines per minute maximum are produced by the other printers, a line printer will operate up to 3,000 lines per minute.

[8] There are several types of non-impact printers called **thermal** and **electrosensitive printers** (**electrostatic printers**). These printers use a special chemically treated paper and expose the characters onto it by some means such as a laser. The characters are then fixed onto the paper by heating it. Because the printing element is simple and has no moving parts, these printers are inexpensive and silent. These newer devices are also much faster and allow any character set to be used. In addition to drawing lines and shading, light can be flashed through a translucent slide to expose a drawing onto the paper. Very fast non-impact printers are capable of rates up to 13,360 lines per minute.

[9] In the largest computer installations, where cost is no longer a consideration, non-impact printers are used for very high speed. An **ink jet** printer operates by projecting small ink droplets and deflecting them electrostatically. Speeds of 40,000 lines per minute may be achieved. In

the **laser writer**, the paper is charged electrostatically and attracts dry ink powder, as in a Xerox machine. The pattern is then baked in the paper. Many lines are printed simultaneously, and speeds of 20,000 lines per minute can be attained.

[10] Multiple copies of output are often required, and can be produced either by printing the report several times or by using multipart paper, which consists of layers of paper separated by carbon sheets. However, non-impact printers cannot use such multipart paper.

[11] Microfilm is often used as an alternative to the printer. The output is 'printed' on microfilm rather than paper, which, in addition to being faster, also condenses large stacks of paper down into small amounts of microfilm with no special programming. The drawback of computer-output microfilm (COM) is that it takes a special device to print the microfilm and a special viewer to read it.

Exercises

1 Main idea

Which statement best expresses the main idea of the text? Why did you eliminate the other choices?

☐ 1. Line printers are the most superior of the impact printers because they are the fastest.

☐ 2. Basically, there are two types of printers: impact and non-impact.

☐ 3. Microfilm is replacing the printer because it is a faster way of storing information.

2 Understanding the passage

Decide whether the following statements are true or false (T/F) by referring to the information in the text. Then make the necessary changes so that the false statements become true.

T F

☐ ☐ 1. A printed output of the data-processing operations is valuable because it provides a permanent record of the results.

☐ ☐ 2. Chain and train printers give a better quality printing than drum printers.

Unit 16 Printers

T	F	
☐	☐	3. Drum printers move sideways across the page.
☐	☐	4. The matrix printer is excellent for business letters because the print is very clear.
☐	☐	5. Line printers are much faster than other impact printers.
☐	☐	6. Line printers print one complete word at a time.
☐	☐	7. Thermal and electrostatic printers are capable of shading, whereas impact printers are not.
☐	☐	8. Where speed is required, line printers are used.
☐	☐	9. Laser writers are capable of printing more than one line at a time.
☐	☐	10. Computer microfilm is printed using the regular printer.

3 Locating information

Find the passages in the text where the following ideas are expressed. Give the line references.

.... 1. With this machine, it is possible to print many lines at the same time.
.... 2. The paper is heated in order to fix the characters on it.
.... 3. Printers may be classified into two main types.
.... 4. These printers are relatively inexpensive, have a high speed and are quiet, but produce poor quality printing.
.... 5. The poorest quality printing is from drum printers.

4 Contextual reference

Look back at the text and find out what the words in **bold** typeface refer to.

1. **It** is two dimensional   (l. 2) ....
2. **they** have definite ideas   (l. 6) ....
3. after seeing **it** there   (l. 7) ....
4. **it** is hammered   (l. 22) ....
5. **each** being on an individual arm (l. 35) ....
6. a coil, **which**, when energized (l. 42) ....
7. **that** make up the words   (l. 62) ....
8. **which** consists of layers   (l. 86) ....
9. than paper, **which**, in addition (l. 89) ....
10. a special viewer to read **it**   (l. 93) ....

5 Understanding words

Refer back to the text and find synonyms for the following words.

1. hitting (l. 17) ....
2. correct or suitable (l. 22) ....
3. draws to or pulls towards (l. 80) ....
4. at the same time (l. 82) ....
5. disadvantage (l. 91) ....

Now refer back to the text and find antonyms for the following words.

6. simple (l. 10) ....
7. temporary (l. 12) ....
8. non-impact (l. 18) ....
9. unreliable (l. 38) ....
10. hide (l. 74) ....

6 Word forms

First choose the appropriate form of the words to complete the sentences. Then check the differences of meaning in your dictionary.

1. appearance, appear, appearing
   a. The first real calculating machine .... in 1820 as the result of several people's experiments.
   b. The .... of new microcomputer systems on the market has increased the competition, forcing the prices down.

2. rotation, rotate, rotating, rotator
   a. When a line printer is in print mode, the cylinder with the characters starts ....
   b. The plotter .... to allow drawing circular designs.
   c. The daisy wheel printer uses a wheel with up to 100 characters, each being on an individual arm, so that only .... is needed for printing.

3. revolution, revolve, revolved, revolving
   a. Certain impact printers have cylinders with the characters set on them which .... in order to print a line.
   b. In this process, one complete line of characters is printed during one .... of the cylinder.
   c. The entrance of the new computer centre has a .... door.

4. installation, instalment, install, installing

   a. .... a computer in a company is the work of technicians and engineers.
   b. Our technicians helped .... a microcomputer system in the language school.
   c. The computer .... at the University has an IBM-370 and many peripherals.

7a Content review

Match the following words in column A with the corresponding information in column B.

	A	B
☐	1. impact	a. characters move sideways
☐	2. drum	b. patterns of dots are printed
☐	3. chain	c. prints all the 'Ds' in a line before all the 'Es'
☐	4. daisy wheel printer	
☐	5. matrix printer	d. heat used to print characters on paper
☐	6. line printer	e. uses dry ink powder
☐	7. thermal printer	f. uses special paper which is treated chemically
☐	8. electrosensitive printer	
☐	9. ink jet printer	g. uses drops of ink
☐	10. laser writer	h. printing by striking characters through a carbon
		i. one cylinder for every character position
		j. 100 arms, each with a different character

7b Content review

First summarize the text on 'Printers' by completing the following table.

		CHARACTERISTICS	QUALITY
IMPACT	Drum	spinning cylinder for each character position; cylinder contains all characters	low quality; characters may be above or below line
	Chain or train		
	Daisy wheel		superb print quality; fast and quiet
	Matrix		
	Line	cylinder with segments each having the full set of characters in raised form	
NON-IMPACT	Thermal electrosensitive		
OTHERS	Ink jet		very fast – up to 40,000 lines per minute
	Laser		
	Microfilm	requires special device for printing and special view for reading	

Unit 16 Printers

Now indicate the kind of printer that corresponds to the given information.

1. .... moves characters sideways
2. .... prints patterns of data for characters
3. .... prints all the 'Ds' in a line before all the 'Es'
4. .... uses heat to print characters on paper
5. .... uses dry ink powder
6. .... uses special paper which is treated chemically
7. .... uses drops of ink
8. .... has 100 arms, each with a different character
9. .... has one cylinder for every character position
10. .... prints by striking characters through a carbon

8 Focus review

Focus F   Comparisons

The following sentences were taken from Unit 16, 'Printers'. Decide whether the sentences express: a. equivalence; b. non-equivalence; or c. the superlative, then underline the words expressing the comparison.

.... 1. One of the most difficult parts of printing output is the reaction of the

.... 2. user to the printed page, because somehow the printed output produces a response from the reader much like that of people to a roomful of new furniture.

.... 3. Drum printers usually give the lowest quality printing because if the hammer hits a little early or late, the character will appear slightly above or below the line.

.... 4. Electrosensitive printers are inexpensive and silent, and these newer devices are also much faster, allowing any character set to be used.

.... 5. In the largest computer installations, where cost is no longer a consideration, non-impact printers are used for very high speed.

.... 6. In addition to being faster, microfilm also condenses large stacks of paper down into small amounts.

.... 7. In the laser writer, the paper is charged electrostatically and attracts dry ink powder, as in a Xerox machine.

Focus H   Giving examples
Complete the following table by referring back to the text on 'Printers'.

PARA	ITEM TO BE EXEMPLIFIED	EXAMPLE MARKER	EXAMPLE
[1]		for instance	
[7]	Segments		
[8]			laser

Focus J   Giving an explanation or a definition
In the following sentences taken from the text on 'Printers', underline the part of the sentence which gives an explanation or definition, then circle the term which is being explained or defined.

1. There are two ways of printing: by impact (striking a character through a carbon, like a typewriter) or non-impact (photocopying, like an office copier).
2. All segments are aligned with one another, that is, all the 'A's, for example are in line.
3. Multiple copies of output are often required, and can be produced either by printing the report several times or by using multipart paper, which consists of layers of paper separated by carbon sheets.

Focus L   Contrasting
Now read 'Printers' (Unit 16) again and, while reading, complete the table below.

PARA	CONTRASTIVE MARKERS	ITEMS CONTRASTED
[1]	but	
[6]		daisy wheel/matrix
[6]	however	
[7]		line printers/others
[10]	however	

UNIT 17

Terminals

[1] As central computers became faster and more powerful, it was possible to establish many remote display stations from which operators could all use the same computer to display information and enter data. Later, even the small machines were equipped with a fairly large **display screen** and **keyboard** oriented towards use by a person with limited training, rather than by a highly skilled computer operator.

[2] For many interactions with computers a permanent record is unnecessary; therefore, output that is scanned once and then thrown away produces a lot of wasted paper. To solve this problem **cathode ray tube (CRT)** terminals can be used. In addition to eliminating paper waste, these terminals are completely silent and frequently much faster than **hard-copy** terminals. Because of their speed and quietness, CRT terminals are very useful **interactive** devices for use in offices and in other areas. The electronic circuitry used in them is very much the same as that in the familiar TV (video) set.

[3] These display terminals are diverse and colourful. The original video output was single-colour (black and white) upper-case letters, but in more highly developed devices, lower-case letters can be displayed, and some give options of blinking and **dual-density** characters. Certain screens can produce 'negative' (dark) characters on a bright background or even make each character a different colour, if so desired. The latter is an important feature in order to catch someone's attention when a value is abnormal.

[4] More sophisticated screens can generate continuous lines for graphic displays. The simplest of these are **monochromatic** and may have strictly limited graphic applications. For example, they may use special characters strung together in order to form lines that look continuous, or they may be restricted regarding the number and the shape of curves that can be drawn at once. Multicolour pictorial graphics are extremely useful in emphasizing contrast, and have been used with good results in nuclear medicine, where differences in intensity would be too subtle if shades of only one colour were used.

[5] The full power of visual display terminals may soon be realized. Already **dynamic** (motion) **graphics** output devices that display simple changing scenes have been developed for flight trainers and computer-generated

movies. These devices could have an important impact on the use of **computer-assisted instruction** (CAI) techniques in schools and colleges.

[6] Besides screens, a wide variety of devices called **plotters** are used to produce permanent copies of graphic output. The first plotters developed used a pen that moved back and forth across the rotating drum to which paper was attached. These devices produced results which were both quite accurate and reasonably fast. Other plotters featuring a moving pen in two dimensions are relatively slow, because not only are they mechanical devices, but most can produce only one continuous line at a time. However, the modern **electrostatic plotter**, an extension of the previously mentioned electrostatic printer, can obtain slightly less artistic results in seconds because it doesn't depend on a moving pen. This is because it electronically generates patterns of dots in a line across the page to make up a picture.

[7] Graphic output may be an effective alternative to high-speed hard-copy output where graphs are more useful than columns of numbers for showing results. Most of the time, a graph is not only better than columns and pages of printed numbers, but also has the advantages of being quicker to produce and easier to understand and file. Pen plotters have been used a great deal in scientific research, where results are often expressed in terms of graphs.

[8] In recent years, new output devices have been developed to bridge the gaps between the various devices just described. For instance, terminals with both video screen and hard-copy output are now available. These devices don't waste paper, since hard copy is produced only when a permanent record is needed. Terminals of this nature are used in applications where relevant personal data is needed which can be corrected or edited on a screen before a hard copy is made. University registration or patient registration are two areas where these devices save time and money, because a new hard copy need be produced only if something has changed from the previous registration or visit.

[9] Finally, there are electrostatic printer-plotters available which produce both print and graphic displays with equal facility. It is possible with these devices to change the style and size of the letters at the users' wish and to have graphs and displays interspersed between the printed lines.

[10] It is therefore very clear that in modern times, the converging technologies of printers, plotters, and graphic displays have resulted in the creation of a few hybrid devices capable of doing many things.

Unit 17 Terminals

Exercises

1 Main idea

Which statement best expresses the main idea of the text? Why did you eliminate the other choices?

☐ 1. CRT terminals are interactive peripheral devices which allow users access to the computer even from remote stations.

☐ 2. Modern terminals have numerous features which can be of use in computer-assisted instruction.

☐ 3. Some modern terminals are equipped with video screen and hard copy output.

2 Understanding the passage

Decide whether the following statements are true or false (T/F) by referring to the information in the text. Then make the necessary changes so that the false statements become true.

T F

☐ ☐ 1. The development of CRT terminals helped reduce the problem of wasted paper.

☐ ☐ 2. Blinking is one of the features which display terminals are incapable of.

☐ ☐ 3. Multicolour graphs are more useful in modern medicine than monochromatic graphs.

☐ ☐ 4. Plotters can move in various directions, but the majority produce one continuous line at a time.

☐ ☐ 5. All plotters depend on a moving pen.

☐ ☐ 6. Terminals with video screens and hard copy output are useful for checking student records.

☐ ☐ 7. Terminals are considered peripheral devices but plotters are not.

☐ ☐ 8. Both interactive terminals and plotters have to be on-line at all times.

☐ ☐ 9. On modern terminals, it is possible to display both upper and lower-case letters.

☐ ☐ 10. Dynamic graphics were first developed for computer-assisted instruction (CAI).

3 Locating information

Find the passages in the text where the following ideas are expressed. Give the line references.

.... 1. Some screens are capable of drawing continuous lines in graphic representations.
.... 2. Hybrid devices that can do what individual printers, plotters, and graphic display units can do are now available.
.... 3. It is not essential to have a printout of every interaction with the computer.
.... 4. Hospitals and universities can benefit from devices that combine a video screen and a hard-copy output.
.... 5. Coloured graphics have been used in the field of medicine.

4 Contextual reference

Look back at the text and find out what the words in **bold** typeface refer to.

1. Because of **their** speed (l. 12) ....
2. and **some** give options (l. 19) ....
3. The **latter** is an important feature (l. 21) ....
4. The simplest of **these** are monochromatic (l. 25) ....
5. curves **that** can be drawn (l. 29) ....
6. not only are **they** mechanical (l. 44) ....
7. **This** is because it (l. 48) ....
8. applications **where** relevant personal (l. 62) ....
9. is needed **which** can be corrected (l. 62) ....
10. **which** produce both print (l. 67) ....

5 Understanding words

Refer back to the text and find synonyms for the following words.

1. distant   (l. 2)   ....
2. get   (l. 47) ....
3. kind   (l. 61) ....
4. ease   (l. 68) ....
5. scattered   (l. 70) ....

Now refer back to the text and find antonyms for the following words.

6. extensive   (l. 5)   ....
7. normal   (l. 23) ....
8. broken   (l. 24) ....
9. unlimited   (l. 28) ....
10. unable   (l. 73) ....

6 Word forms

First choose the appropriate form of the words to complete the sentences. Then check the differences of meaning in your dictionary.

1. interaction, interact, interactive
   a. CRT terminals are useful .... devices that allow real-time processing.
   b. Many .... with computers do not require a permanent record; therefore a printed output is unnecessary.
   c. It is very important for students to .... with each other and exchange ideas.

2. restriction, restrict, restricted, restrictive, restrictively
   a. Computer graphic applications are .... by the size of the screen.
   b. A computer has no .... on the number of times it can repeat a mathematical operation.
   c. The computer centre introduced .... measures to stop unauthorized persons from entering the computer room.

3. production, produce, produced, productive, productivity
   a. Plotters are used to .... permanent copies of graphic output.
   b. Dark characters on a bright background can be .... by certain screens.
   c. Computers are used to control mechanical operations in the car industry so as to increase ....

4. development, develop, developed, developing, developer, development
   a. In 1960, the second generation of computers was ....
   b. The future will bring great .... in the mechanical devices associated with computer systems.
   c. .... the chip made it possible for minicomputers and microcomputers to be invented.

5. registration, register, registered, registering
   a. The .... of the control unit temporarily holds instructions read from memory while they are being executed.
   b. New computer owners are .... with our hardware company for one-year maintenance contracts.

7 Content review

Match the following words in column A with the corresponding information in column B.

A
1. interactive
2. display screen
3. hard-copy terminals
4. monochromatic
5. dynamic graphics
6. computer-assisted instruction
7. plotters
8. electrostatic plotters
9. keyboard
10. dual-density

B
a. light and dark of the same colour
b. computer typewriter
c. using the computer in individualized learning
d. pens or devices that draw graphs
e. draws graphs using combinations of dots
f. TV screen of the computer
g. gives paper printouts
h. can ask questions and answers immediately
i. shades of the same colour
j. pictures with motion

8 Focus review

Focus F   Comparisons

Complete the following table by referring back to the text on 'Terminals' (Unit 17).

PARA	EQUIVALENCE	NON-EQUIVALENCE	SUPERLATIVE
[1]			
[2]			
[3]			
[4]			
[6]			

Unit 17 Terminals

PARA	EQUIVALENCE	NON-EQUIVALENCE	SUPERLATIVE
[7]			
[8]			
[9]			

Focus I Adding information

Complete the following table by referring back to the text on 'Terminals' (Unit 17).

PARA	ADDING INFORMATION MARKER	INFORMATION ADDED
[2]		*eliminating paper waste*
[3]	or even	
[4]		*may be restricted regarding the number and the shape of curves that can be drawn*
[6]	besides	
[7]		*has the advantage of being quicker to produce and easier to understand and file*

FOCUS M

Cause and effect

Understanding the different ways of expressing the relationship between the causes and the effects of an action is very important when you are reading English. If an argument begins with *effects* or *results*, the *causes* are the reasons that logically lead to those results. This cause-effect relationship is commonly used in academic texts.

There are many different ways of expressing cause and effect; before looking at some of these ways, note carefully this important distinction:

A   B
CAUSE ⟶ EFFECT   A **results in** B;   A **causes** B

A ⟶ B
Dust **causes** the recording condition of disks to deteriorate.

B   A
EFFECT ⟵ CAUSE   B **results from** A   B **is caused by** A

B   ⟵ A
Deterioration in the recording condition of disks **is caused by** dust.

1 Often, the choice of verbs in a sentence will indicate a cause-effect relationship. The following verbs are used to link a cause with an effect:

result	be caused by
cause	be produced by
produce	result in
allow	result from
prevent	bring about
enable	

Examples

1. The idea of keeping instructions for the computer inside the computer's memory **brought about** significant changes in computer technology. (A ⟶ B)

Focus M Cause and effect

2. In a daisy wheel printer, the hammer hits a single letter, guaranteeing accurate positioning and uniform striking. This **allows** a fast, quiet, and reliable operation, with superb print quality. (A ⟶ B)
3. Dust and dirt **cause** the recording condition of disks to deteriorate. (A ⟶ B)

2 Connectives used in specifying a cause can be any of the following:

> due to
> as the/a result of
> since
> because
> in response to
> as

Examples
1. The first real calculating machines appeared in 1820 **as the result of** several people's experiments. (B ⟵ A)
2. A computer is not a single-purpose machine, **since** instructions can be combined in an infinite number of sequences. (B ⟵ A)
3. **Because** the printing element of line printers is so simple and has no moving parts, these printers are inexpensive and silent. (A ⟶ B)

3 Sentence connectors used in introducing a result are:

> with the result that
> so that
> thus
> therefore
> consequently
> hence
> for this reason

Examples
1. All disks are made of a substance coated with metal oxide and can **therefore** be magnetized.
2. A punch card is organized into 12 rows and 80 columns. **For this reason**, the character is changed into a 12-bit word.
3. The memory of the first computers was made up of fine vertical and horizontal wire. Every intersection had its unique address; **consequently**, when an electrical current was passed through the wires, the cores were identified by their respective addresses.

4 Another way of showing causal relationship is by introducing the cause with **IF**, and both the cause clause and the effect clause verbs are in the present tense.

Examples

1. **If** the necessary information **is located** on secondary memory devices such as disks or tapes, programs and data **are** first **loaded** into internal memory.
2. **If** a tape drive **has** a transfer speed of 200 IPS, reading from a 6250 BPI density tape **is like reading** 15,000 cards in one second.

Exercise 1

Read the following sentences and underline that part which expresses the **cause**.

1. **Because** electric pulses can move at the speed of light, a computer can carry out vast numbers of arithmetic-logical operations almost instantaneously. (Unit 1, paragraph 5)
2. People went on using some form of abacus well into the 16th century, and it is still being used in some parts of the world **because** it can be understood without knowing how to read. (Unit 2, paragraph 1)
3. When computers fail, it is **due to** human error and not the fault of computers. (Unit 4, paragraph 4)
4. Most primary memory is costly, and **therefore** it is used transiently. (Unit 10, paragraph 2)
5. A keypunch is not physically connected to the computer in any way; **hence,** it is said to be off-line. (Unit 3, paragraph 2)

Now read the following sentences and underline that part which expresses the **effect/result**.

1. Computers can remove many of the routine and boring tasks from our lives, **thereby** leaving us with more time for interesting, creative work. (Unit 3, paragraph 6)
2. **Because** they are man-made machines, computers sometimes malfunction or break down and have to be repaired. (Unit 7, paragraph 3)
3. **Since** the operating environment for most minicomputers is far less varied and more complex than for large mainframes, their software and peripheral requirements differ greatly. (Unit 7, paragraph 3)
4. Random-access devices bypass large amounts of irrelevant data, and **therefore** reduce access time considerably. (Unit 10, paragraph 4)

Focus M Cause and effect

5. Mainframes have been reduced in both size and cost **as a result of** advances made in the manufacturing of miniaturized circuitry. (Unit 2, paragraph 2)

Exercise 2
Complete the following table by referring back to the text on 'Printers', (Unit 16).

PARA	MARKER	CAUSE	EFFECT/RESULT
[1]	*Occurs*		
[3]		*each cylinder spins into the appropriate character position*	
[4]			*it is hammered onto the paper through a carbon ribbon*
[5]	*allows*		
[6]		*the inertia is minimal*	
[7]			*the character on the cylinder segment is brought into contact with the ribbon and paper*
[8]	*because*		

180 Focus M Cause and effect

Exercise 3
Refer back to paragraphs 2 and 6 of 'Terminals' (Unit 17) and complete the table below.

PARA	MARKER	CAUSE	EFFECT/RESULT
[2]	*therefore*		
		speed and quietness	
[6]			*results were accurate and fast*
	because		
		doesn't depend on moving pen	

PART 3

Data processing

Data processing refers to the operations which are performed on the data either to derive information from them or to order them in files. These operations include functions performed both by programmers and by automatic equipment.

The functions of programmers are to prepare, test, and document computer programs. This step encompasses analysing a problem, formulating an algorithm to solve it, translating the algorithm into a high-level language, testing the program, and running it with the data. The functions of the computer, on the other hand, are to perform arithmetic and logical operations on the program and data after they have been translated to machine code, and to make the results of these operations accessible to humans.

Data may be processed in batch or in real time. The former means grouping transactions and processing them as one unit, while the latter refers to processing the data almost simultaneously as it is generated. Another approach to data processing is structuring and organizing the data so as to make them useful and available to more than one particular user. This is called data base management.

SECTION 7
Programming

UNIT 18

Steps in problem solving

[1] Can a computer solve problems? Definitely not. It is a machine that carries out the procedures which the programmer gives it. It is the programmer then who solves the problems. There are a few steps that one has to follow in problem solving:

[2] Step 1. The programmer must define the problem clearly. This means that he or she has to determine, in a general way, how to solve the problem. Some problems are easy, while others take months of study. The programmer should always start by asking: 'Do I understand the problem?'.

[3] Step 2. The programmer must formulate an **algorithm**, which is a straightforward sequence of steps of instructions used to solve the problem. Constructing an algorithm is the most important part of problem solving and is usually time-consuming. An algorithm can be described by a **flowchart**, which may be stated in terms of a sequence of precise sentences, or a **block diagram**. The latter is a diagrammatic representation of the sequence of events to be followed in solving the problem. The relationship between the events is shown by means of a connecting arrow -----→. A block diagram can show if a process has to be repeated or if there are alternative routes to be taken.

[4] Step 3. The programmer must translate the algorithm or flowchart into a computer program. To do so, he or she writes detailed instructions for the computer, using one of the many computer languages available following the exact sequence of the flowchart algorithm. The program is usually written on **coding sheets** which have a specific format drawn on them.

[5] Step 4. The programmer must then keypunch the program, or give the coding sheets to the keypunch operator to do it. The program is either punched on cards or entered into the computer at a terminal with a visual display unit.

[6] Step 5. The program must then be tested. To do so, the computer operator puts the deck of cards in the card reader and presses the 'read' button. This transfers the information to the memory of the computer. Next, a printout shows if the program works or if it has errors (called **bugs**). If the programmer is using a terminal instead of cards to enter the instructions it is possible, with the aid of a few commands, to store the program in the memory of the computer and get a **printout**.

[7] Step 6. The last step is to add the data to the program and run the job completely. The computer will then perform the calculations necessary to solve the problem. It will follow the instructions in the program to the minutest details. Therefore, one can say that the computer is a **robot**. It doesn't think, but simply does what it is told.

Exercises

1 Main idea

Which statement best expresses the main idea of the text? Why did you eliminate the other choices?

☐ 1. Constructing an algorithm is the basic step in solving a problem.

☐ 2. Solving problems becomes easier if certain steps are followed.

☐ 3. The computer does what the programmer tells it to do.

2 Understanding the passage

Decide whether the following statements are true or false (T/F) by referring to the information in the text. Then make the necessary changes so that the false statements become true.

T F

☐ ☐ 1. The computer is a great help to people because it solves their problems.

☐ ☐ 2. All problems are equally difficult to solve.

☐ ☐ 3. An algorithm is a sequence of instructions used to solve a problem.

☐ ☐ 4. The most important part of problem solving is defining the problem clearly.

☐ ☐ 5. Block diagrams cannot show relationships.

☐ ☐ 6. Coding sheets are used for writing programs.

☐ ☐ 7. Punched cards are the only way of transferring the program to the computer memory.

☐ ☐ 8. If the data is not added to the program, the computer cannot perform calculations.

☐ ☐ 9. It is a good idea to test the program before adding the data.

☐ ☐ 10. A computer is very intelligent. It is capable of thinking.

3 Locating information

Find the passages in the text where the following ideas are expressed. Give the line references.

.... 1. Programs are usually written on certain lined forms.
.... 2. A block diagram can show a decision with two different outcomes.
.... 3. The programmer is the one who solves the problems.
.... 4. Even if the programmer is using a terminal instead of cards, it is possible to get a permanent copy of his program.
.... 5. Not all problems are of the same level of difficulty.

4 Contextual reference

Look back at the text and find out what the words in **bold** typeface refer to.

1. **It** is a machine (l. 1) ....
2. **which** the programmer gives it (l. 2) ....
3. **who** solves the problems (l. 3) ....
4. **which** may be stated (l. 14) ....
5. The **latter** is a diagrammatic representation (l. 15) ....
6. operator to do **it** (l. 27) ....
7. **This** transfers the information (l. 32) ....
8. or if **it** has errors (l. 33) ....
9. **It** will follow the instructions (l. 40) ....
10. does what **it** is told (l. 42) ....

5 Understanding words

Refer back to the text and find synonyms for the following words.

1. construct (l. 10) ....
2. takes a lot of time (l. 13) ....
3. exact (l. 15) ....
4. mistakes (l. 34) ....
5. help (l. 35) ....

Now refer back to the text and find antonyms for the following words.

6. ambiguously (l. 5) ....
7. specific (l. 6) ....
8. partially (l. 39) ....

6 Word forms

First choose the appropriate form of the words to complete the sentences. Then check the differences of meaning in your dictionary.

1. procedure, proceed, proceeding
    a. The machine carries out the .... which the programmer gives it.
    b. You should .... with care when using a calculator.

2. program, programmer, programmed, programming
    a. I would like to .... in COBOL.
    b. There were quite a few errors in my ....
    c. My calculator is .... It plays a tune on the hour.
    d. Fortran is one of the many .... languages available on the market.
    e. Computer .... is a new field of study at the university.
    f. He is a good .... because he always constructs algorithms for his problems.

3. relationship, relate, related
    a. The first two steps in your program are not .... They are basically different.
    b. In a flowchart, the .... between events is shown by means of connecting arrows.

4. code, coding
    a. Do you have any .... sheets left?
    b. I have to .... my program.
    c. Assembler is one example of a machine ....

5. printer, printing, print, printed
    a. .... your name and address in block letters.
    b. .... was introduced by Gutenberg in Germany in the 1400s.
    c. The quality of the .... output from a daisy wheel printer is superior to that from a dot matrix.
    d. .... provide a hard copy of the results of data processing operations.

7a Content review

Try to think of a definition for each of these items before checking them in the Glossary. Then complete the following statements with the appropriate words. Make sure you use the correct form, i.e. singular or plural.

| algorithm | coding sheets | flowchart |
| robot | printout | bugs |

1. Special forms which are usually used for writing programs are called ....
2. Another word for program errors is ....
3. A number of steps used in solving a program is called an ....
4. A machine which is incapable of thinking but follows instructions is called a ....
5. A .... is either a group of exact sentences to solve a problem or a block diagram.

7b Content review

Solving a problem is a process involving various steps. Complete the following diagram to show the sequence of these steps.

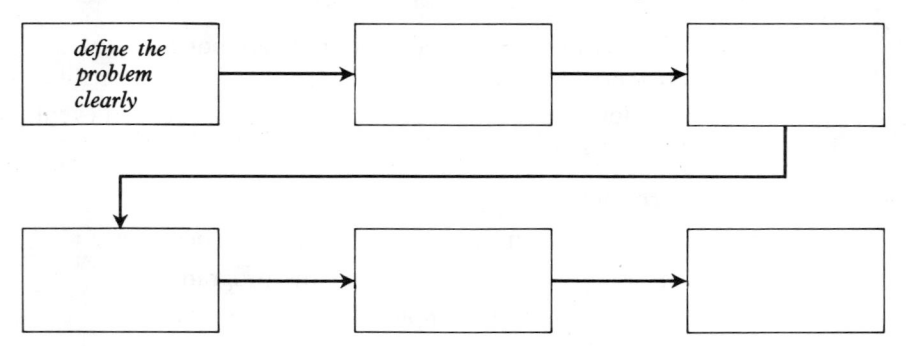

[Diagram: define the problem clearly → □ → □ → □ → □ → □]

8 Focus review

Focus M Cause and effect/result

The following sentences were taken from the text on 'Steps in Problem Solving'. While reading these sentences, underline the cause once, the effect/result twice, then circle the *causal-effect/result marker*.

1. If the programmer is using a terminal instead of cards to enter his instructions, he can, with the aid of a few commands, store the program in the memory of the computer and get a printout.
2. The computer will follow the instructions in the program to the minutest details. Therefore, one can say that the computer is a robot.

UNIT 19

Computer arithmetic

[1] The digital computer is an electronic machine which contains thousands of tiny circuits characterized by the fact that they have only two states: complete and broken. A complete circuit signifies that the electricity is *on*, whereas a broken circuit signifies that the electricity is *off*. It is through the on and off states that information is transmitted by the computer. Substituting numbers for these states, one can say that 1 is on and 0 is off; this is the number system on which the computer operates. Because there are only two digits in this system, it is termed a **binary** system with the 0 and 1 being called **bits** — B from binary and **it** from digit. They can represent all other numbers, the alphabet, and special characters such as $ and #.

[2] In our everyday arithmetic, we use the **decimal** system, which is based on ten digits — 0, 1, 2, 3, 4, 5, 6, 7, 8, and 9. In the decimal system, multiplication by ten would yield the following results:

$$10 = (10^0 \times 0) + (10^1 \times 1)$$
$$100 = (10^0 \times 0) + (10^1 \times 0) + (10^2 \times 1)$$
$$1000 = (10^0 \times 0) + (10^1 \times 0) + (10^2 \times 1) + (10^3 \times 1)$$

In tabulating this, we notice that we multiply by 10 each time we move a number one column to the left; that is, we increase the base number 10 by the power 1.

(10^3)	(10^2)	(10^1)	(10^0)	
1000	100	10	1	
			1	(1)
		1	0	(10)
	1	0	0	(100)
1	0	0	0	(1000)

Therefore, 652 in the decimal system is equal to 2 + 50 + 600:

100	10	1	
		2	(1×2)
	5	0	(10×5)
6	0	0	(100×6)

[3] Since the binary system is based on two digits, 0 and 1, we multiply by 2 instead of by 10 each time we move a number one column to the left. So to convert binary to decimal, we use the base number 2 with sequentially increasing powers.

(2^3) (2^2) (2^1) (2^0)
8   4   2   2

As an example, the decimal number 1 is 0001 in binary.

8	4	2	1	(decimal)
0	0	0	1	(1×1)

The decimal number 2 is equal to 1×2 plus 0×1 or 0010 in binary.

8	4	2	1	
0	0	1	0	(0×1) plus (1×2)

The decimal number 3 is equal to 1×1 plus 1×2 or 0011 in binary.

8	4	2	1
0	0	1	1

Let us tabulate the decimal numbers 0 to 15 in the binary system.

(2^3)	(2^2)	(2^1)	(2^0)	
8	4	2	1	
0	0	0	0	(0)
0	0	0	1	(1)
0	0	1	0	(2)
0	0	1	1	(3)
0	1	0	0	(4)
0	1	0	1	(5)
0	1	1	0	(6)
0	1	1	1	(7)
1	0	0	0	(8)
1	0	0	1	(9)
1	0	1	0	(10)
1	0	1	1	(11)
1	1	0	0	(12)
1	1	0	1	(13)
1	1	1	0	(14)
1	1	1	1	(15)

[4] The binary system is very tedious for humans, especially in the handling of long numbers, and this increases the possibility of committing errors. To overcome this limitation, two number systems were developed which are used as a form of shorthand in reading groups of four binary digits. These are the **octal** system with a base of 8, and the **hexadecimal** system with a base of 16. CDC computers use the octal system, whereas IBM computers use the hexadecimal.

[5] The table above shows that four binary digits may be arranged into 16 different combinations ranging from 0000 to 1111. This forms the basis of the hexadecimal system. To represent these binary combinations, the system uses the digits 0 to 9 and 6 letters of the alphabet: A, B, C, D, E, and F. Following is a table that shows the relationship between the binary, the octal, the hexadecimal, and the decimal systems.

Decimal	Hexadecimal	Octal	Binary
0	0	0	0000
1	1	1	0001
2	2	2	0010
3	3	3	0011
4	4	4	0100
5	5	5	0101
6	6	6	0110
7	7	7	0111
8	8	10	1000
9	9	11	1001
10	A	12	1010
11	B	13	1011
12	C	14	1100
13	D	15	1101
14	E	16	1110
15	F	17	1111

[6] On some computers, addition is the only arithmetic operation possible. The remaining arithmetic operations are based on the operation of addition (+): subtraction (−) can be thought of as the addition of negative numbers; multiplication (×) is repeated addition; division (÷) is repeated subtraction. How do we add in the binary system? There are four basic rules of addition which we must remember:

$1 + 0 = 1$
$0 + 1 = 1$
$0 + 0 = 0$
$1 + 1 = 0$ and carry 1 or 10 (read from the right to the left as zero–one).

Here is an example:

Binary	Decimal
1110	14
1000	8
10110	22

Exercises

1 Main idea
Which statement best expresses the main idea of the text? Why did you eliminate the other choices?

☐ 1. There are four different number systems.

☐ 2. Most arithmetic operations can be analysed in terms of addition.

☐ 3. Computer arithmetic is based on 0 and 1.

2 Understanding the passage
Decide whether the following statements are true or false (T/F) by referring to the information in the text. Then make the necessary changes so that the false statements become true.

T F

☐ ☐ 1. The digital computer uses the decimal number system.

☐ ☐ 2. In the decimal system, the 0 is called a bit.

☐ ☐ 3. The binary system has only two digits.

☐ ☐ 4. In binary arithmetic $1 + 1 = 0$.

☐ ☐ 5. Unlike IBM computers, CDC computer arithmetic is based on 8 digits.

☐ ☐ 6. The hexadecimal system is based on 16 numbers.

☐ ☐ 7. To subtract a number really means to add a negative number.

☐ ☐ 8. The computer transmits information through the principle of connected or broken electrical circuits.

☐ ☐ 9. The $ sign cannot be represented in the binary system because it is not a number.

☐ ☐ 10. The hexadecimal system is an economical way of representing the binary system.

3 Locating information
Find the passages in the text where the following ideas are expressed. Give the line references.

.... 1. To do calculations using the binary system is laborious work.
.... 2. The computer gets information by means of electric circuits which are either on or off.
.... 3. In binary, $1 + 1$ equals 0 and 1 is carried to the next column.

Unit 19 Computer arithmetic

.... 4. Both numbers and letters are used in the hexadecimal system.
.... 5. The binary system has two digits only.

4 Contextual reference
Look back at the text and find out what the words in **bold** typeface refer to.

1. that **they** have only two states (l. 2) ....
2. **it** is termed a binary system (l. 8) ....
3. **They** can represent all other numbers (l. 10) ....
4. **which** is based on ten digits (l. 12) ....
5. **this** increases the possibility (l. 67) ....
6. **These** are the octal (l. 70) ....
7. **This** forms the basis (l. 74) ....
8. **that** shows the relationship (l. 77) ....

5 Understanding words
Refer back to the text and find synonyms for the following words.

1. means (l. 3) ....
2. replace (l. 6) ....
3. conditions (l. 6) ....
4. give (l. 14) ....
5. uninteresting (l. 66) ....

Now refer back to the text and find antonyms for the following words.

6. incomplete (l. 3) ....
7. completed circuit (l. 4) ....
8. decrease (l. 19) ....
9. impossibility (l. 67) ....
10. the same (l. 74) ....

6 Word forms
1. characterize, characteristic, characteristically, characterized, character

   a. My daisy wheel printer can print 132 .... per line.
   b. Daisy wheel printers are .... by having a superb print quality.
   c. Can you describe the most important .... of the computer?
   d. The 0 and 1 in computer arithmetic represent the alphabet, all numbers, and special .... such as $ and £.

2. substitution, substituting, substituted, substitute
   a. The 0 and 1 in computer arithmetic are .... for the two states of electricity, i.e. off and on.
   b. There is no .... for the speed at which a computer performs arithmetic operations.

3. conversion, convert, converted, converter
   a. Canada has .... from the British to the metric system. Now centimetres are used instead of inches.
   b. .... from an old computer system to a new one can be time-consuming and complicated.
   c. Before the computer can do the necessary computations for a problem, the number should be .... to machine code.

4. combination, combine, combined, combining
   a. To represent the 16 different .... of four binary digits, the hexadecimal system uses the digits 0 to 9 and A, B, C, D, E and F.
   b. Today's microcomputers are almost as powerful as yesterday's minis, mainly because of man's creativity .... with the advancement in chip technology.

5. basis, base, based, basic
   a. The binary system is .... on two digits: 0 and 1.
   b. The decimal system uses 10 as a .... whereas the hexadecimal system uses 16.
   c. Data .... management involves structuring and organizing data so as to make them useful and available to more than one particular user.
   d. Flowcharting is a .... step in programming.

7 Content review

Write the appropriate words for the following definitions.

1. a number system based on 10
2. a number system based on 8
3. a number system based on 16
4. a number system based on 2
5. 0 and 1 when they are the only digits of a number system

UNIT 20

Flowcharting

[1] So far we have dealt mainly with computers, but now it is imperative that we find out how a program is written. In all activities involving computers, it is necessary that the programmer is aware of what the machine is doing and what a program is supposed to do. As previously mentioned, flowcharting, one of the steps in programming, indicates the logical path the computer will follow in **executing** a program; it is a drawing very much like a road map. Flowcharting is not restricted to the preparation of programs in a particular language and should be done for each major problem before the writing of the program is attempted. If the finished program does not run as it should, the errors are more easily detected on the flowchart than in the maze of words, characters, and numbers that make up the computer program. In order to develop a flowchart successfully, a programmer should be aware of the sequence of steps needed to obtain a correct solution to a problem.

[2] There are two ways of making a flowchart: the freehand version and the neater, more readable version. In the former version, the graphic outlines are simply jotted down as the steps of the program are worked out. This is quite satisfactory if the flowchart is not intended to be kept as a permanent record. However, if a permanent, neater and more readable flowchart is needed, the latter method whereby a **template**, a sheet of plastic with all the flowcharting symbols cut into it, is used.

[3] The following symbols should be used for the purpose of uniformity. The first and last symbol is ⬭. This is the **terminal symbol** which indicates the beginning or the end of a program. The word 'START' must be inserted inside the figure if it is the beginning of the program and 'STOP' if it is the end of the program. The figure in the form of a **parallelogram** ▱ is used as an input/output symbol. It indicates that something is either brought to or taken from the program. The **rectangular** symbol ▭ stands for processing and indicates a place in the program where action is taken. In a program, to indicate that a decision has to be made, the diamond-shaped symbol ◇ is used. The decision is usually in the form of a question that must be answered by either 'yes' or 'no'. Finally, the arrows ⟶ are used to show that the flow or direction in which the different actions in the program are performed.

[4] It should be noted that a flowchart is not a program, but only a step in the preparation of a program, and is used in determining how to set up and write the program. However, if the problem is not understood, neither the flowchart nor the program can be done correctly. It is possible for two programmers, working separately, to write programs to solve the same problem and come up with flowcharts and programs that may be altogether different.

[5] After a program has been worked out, it is usually written down and kept with a copy of the flowchart along with detailed instructions for the use and interpretation of the program. This procedure is part of what is referred to as **program documentation**. If documentation isn't available, it is always possible to work backwards and make a flowchart from an application program. It may be necessary to create a new flowchart when the original one is missing, in order to understand the program for which it was a preparatory step.

[6] Flowcharting is one of the first things a student programmer is taught, because a flowchart shows how a person thinks about a problem. In other words, it is through this that a new programmer reveals his or her logical and analytical ability, which is a must in programming.

Exercises

1 Main idea

Which statement expresses the main idea of the text? Why did you eliminate the other choices?

☐ 1. Every programmer must know how to flowchart.

☐ 2. Program documentation specifies what the program is supposed to do.

☐ 3. Flowcharting is a basic step in programming.

2 Understanding the passage

Decide whether the following statements are true or false (T/F) by referring to the information in the text. Then make the necessary changes so that the false statements become true.

T   F

☐ ☐ 1. A good flowchart takes into account the steps which are necessary to solve the problem.

☐ ☐ 2. It is not possible to draw a flowchart without using a template.

Unit 20 *Flowcharting*

T	F	
☐	☐	3. There is only one possible flowchart for every problem.
☐	☐	4. Every programmer must learn flowcharting and realize its importance.
☐	☐	5. The method of flowcharting depends on the programming language being used.
☐	☐	6. Flowcharts show the logic one has to follow to solve a problem.
☐	☐	7. Documenting a program is essential in explaining what the program is supposed to do.
☐	☐	8. If the flowchart is correct, the program will certainly work.
☐	☐	9. Each symbol in flowcharting has a specific meaning.
☐	☐	10. Flowcharts can show processes, but not decisions.

3 Locating information

Find the passages in the text where the following ideas are expressed. Give the line references.

.... 1. A programmer must document his program in order that others may be able to understand it.
.... 2. Flowcharting resembles a map.
.... 3. Flowcharting shows the logical ability of a programmer.
.... 4. There is more than one way of flowcharting.
.... 5. A certain symbol is used to indicate if a question is to be answered 'yes' or 'no'.

4 Contextual reference

Look back at the text and find out what the words in **bold** typeface refer to.

1. does not run as **it** should (l. 10) ....
2. In the **former** version (l. 16) ....
3. **This** is quite satisfactory (l. 18) ....
4. the **latter** method (l. 20) ....
5. flowcharting symbols cut into **it** (l. 21) ....
6. **which** indicates the beginning (l. 23) ....
7. **It** indicates that something (l. 27) ....
8. **that** may be altogether different (l. 40) ....
9. the original **one** is missing (l. 48) ....
10. **which** is a must in programming (l. 53) ....

5 Understanding words

Refer back to the text and find synonyms for the following words.

1. route   (l. 6)   ....
2. try   (l. 9)   ....
3. answer   (l. 14) ....
4. put in   (l. 25) ....
5. show   (l. 52) ....

Now refer back to the text and find antonyms for the following words.

6. unlimited   (l. 7)   ....
7. undiscovered   (l. 11) ....
8. temporary   (l. 19) ....
9. inaccessible   (l. 45) ....
10. illogical   (l. 53) ....

6 Word forms

First choose the appropriate form of the words to complete the sentence. Then check the differences of meaning in your dictionary.

1. involvement, involve, involved, involving

    a. In most operations .... calculations, computers can do the job much faster than man.
    b. Flowcharting .... a logical analysis of a problem and a diagrammatic representation of the sequence of events to be followed in solving the problem.
    c. The .... of the new programmer in the user's group was appreciated by his manager.

2. correction, correct, corrected, corrective, correcting

    a. It is always a good approach to .... the errors in your program before running it with the data.
    b. In order to develop a good flowchart, a programmer should be aware of the sequence of steps needed to obtain a .... solution to a problem.
    c. He submitted the .... version of the program to be keypunched.

3. process, processed, processing

    a. The Central .... Unit is responsible for executing the programs.
    b. A block diagram can show if a .... has to be repeated or if there are alternative routes to be taken.

c. The applications of all the new students were .... by the computer.

4. performance, perform, performed, performing, performer
   a. .... is a verb used quite often in COBOL programming.
   b. Data processing refers to the operations which are .... on the data either to derive information from them or to order them in files.
   c. The .... of the computer salesman was measured by the number of units he sold.

5. documentation, document, documented, documenting
   a. .... a program is essential so that other programmers can understand it.
   b. It took the programmer one week to complete the .... of the programs in the new system.
   c. The payroll package we purchased is very well ....

7a Content review

Try to think of a definition for each of these items before checking them in the Glossary. Then complete the following statements with the appropriate words. Make sure you use the correct form, i.e. singular or plural.

executing	terminal	rectangle
template	parallelogram	diamond
documentation		

1. The information describing what a program can do and what the results mean is referred to as ....
2. It is advisable to test the program without data before .... it.
3. A piece of plastic with different shapes used for flowcharting is called a ....
4. Data used as input must be indicated with a ....
5. The symbol which marks the beginning and end of a program is called the .... symbol.

7b Content review

Problem 1.
Study the following flowchart, which shows the procedure followed in calculating an employee's salary.

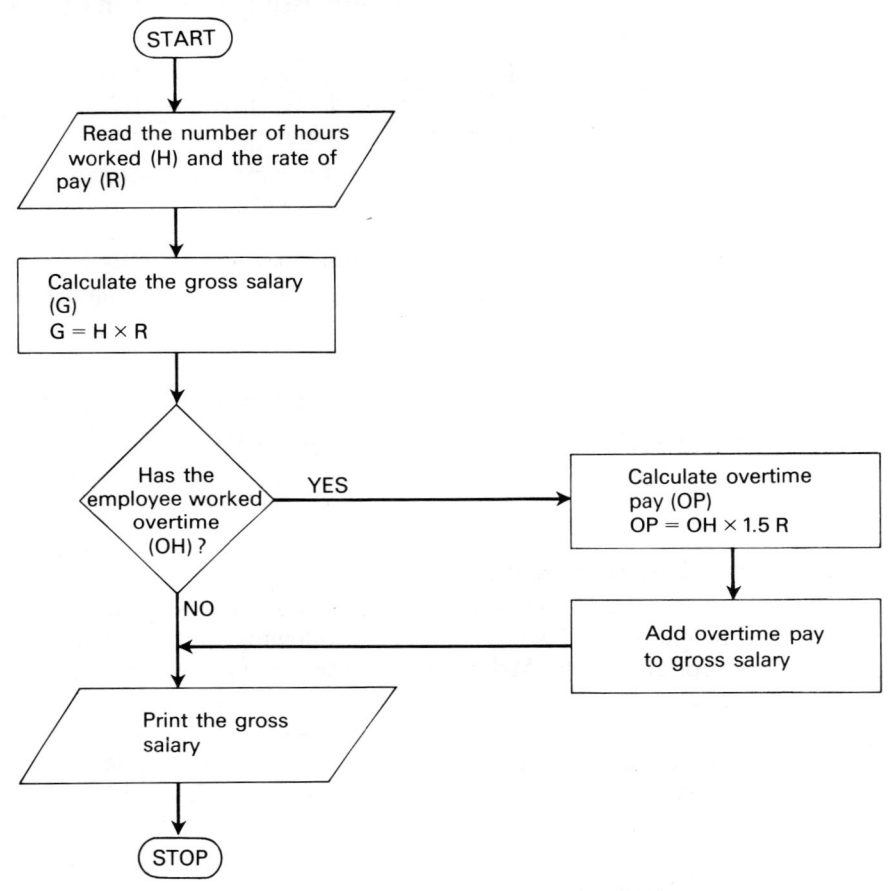

```
                    ( START )
                        │
                        ▼
           ┌──────────────────────────┐
          /  Read the number of hours /
         /   worked (H) and the rate of /
        /    pay (R)                  /
       └──────────────────────────┘
                        │
                        ▼
           ┌──────────────────────────┐
           │ Calculate the gross salary│
           │ (G)                       │
           │ G = H × R                 │
           └──────────────────────────┘
                        │
                        ▼
                   ╱ Has the  ╲      YES         ┌──────────────────────┐
                  ╱  employee  ╲──────────────► │ Calculate overtime    │
                  ╲  worked    ╱                │ pay (OP)              │
                   ╲ overtime ╱                 │ OP = OH × 1.5 R       │
                    ╲ (OH) ? ╱                  └──────────────────────┘
                        │NO                                 │
                        │                                   ▼
                        │                       ┌──────────────────────┐
                        │◄──────────────────────│ Add overtime pay      │
                        │                       │ to gross salary       │
                        ▼                       └──────────────────────┘
           ┌──────────────────────────┐
          /  Print the gross          /
         /   salary                  /
        └──────────────────────────┘
                        │
                        ▼
                    ( STOP )
```

In the following paragraph based on the flowchart above, fill in the blanks with the proper connectives. Use these words: *but, that is, then, if, to begin with, after, first, finally, next, before, in other words.*

In calculating an employee's salary, a computer must go through a number of operations in a logical manner. .... it must read the number of hours worked and the rate of pay for each hour worked. .... it must calculate the gross salary; .... multiply the hours worked by the rate of pay for each hour worked. .... doing these two operations it must find out whether the employee has worked overtime or not. .... he hasn't worked overtime the computer prints out the gross salary. .... if the employee has worked overtime, two more operations are necessary .... printing out the gross salary. .... the overtime pay must be calculated;

.... the number of overtime hours must be multiplied by the overtime rate of pay. .... the overtime pay is added to the gross salary. .... the computer prints out the employee's salary and stops.

Problem 2.
The following flowchart is an example of what many people do before leaving the house everyday. Complete the flowchart by selecting the appropriate event for each step.

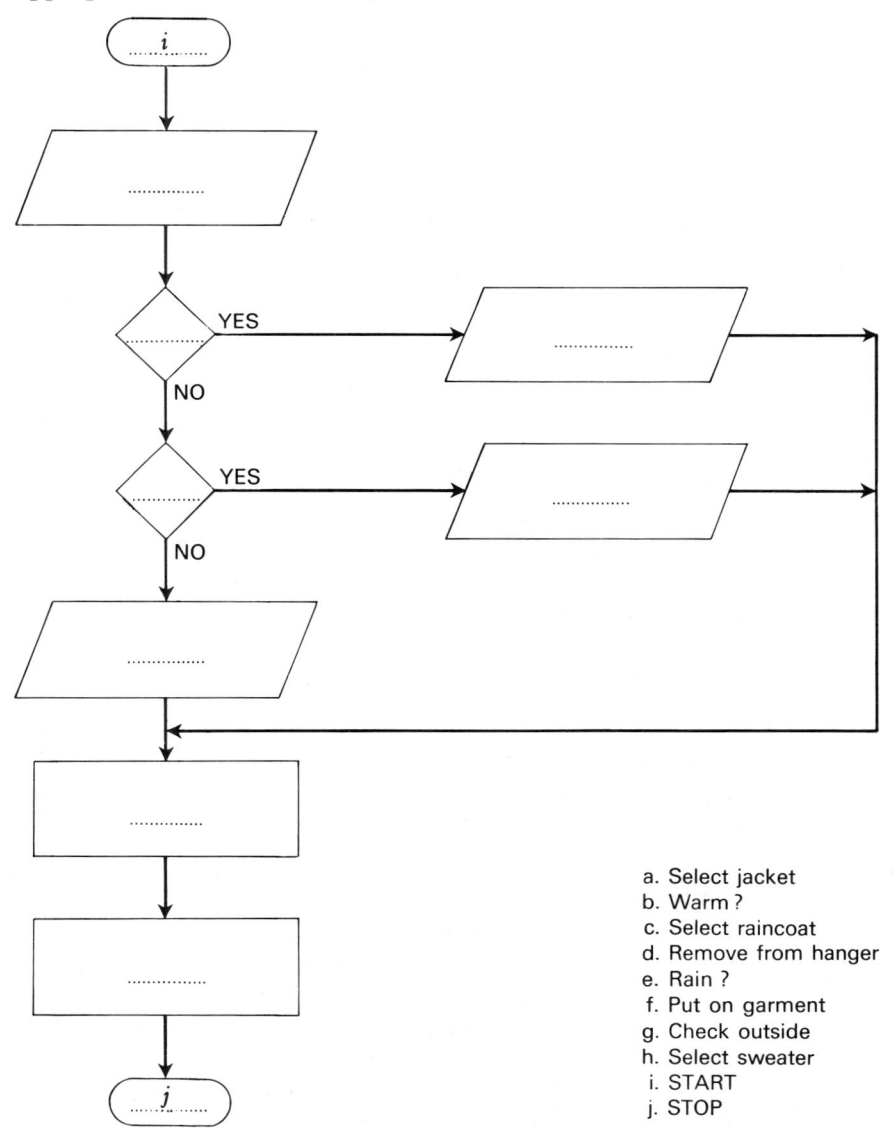

a. Select jacket
b. Warm ?
c. Select raincoat
d. Remove from hanger
e. Rain ?
f. Put on garment
g. Check outside
h. Select sweater
i. START
j. STOP

Problem 3.

In the chemistry laboratory, all glassware is stored in one cupboard. Your instructions are to go to the laboratory and bring back a 300 ml beaker. Flowchart your activities by completing the flowchart below.

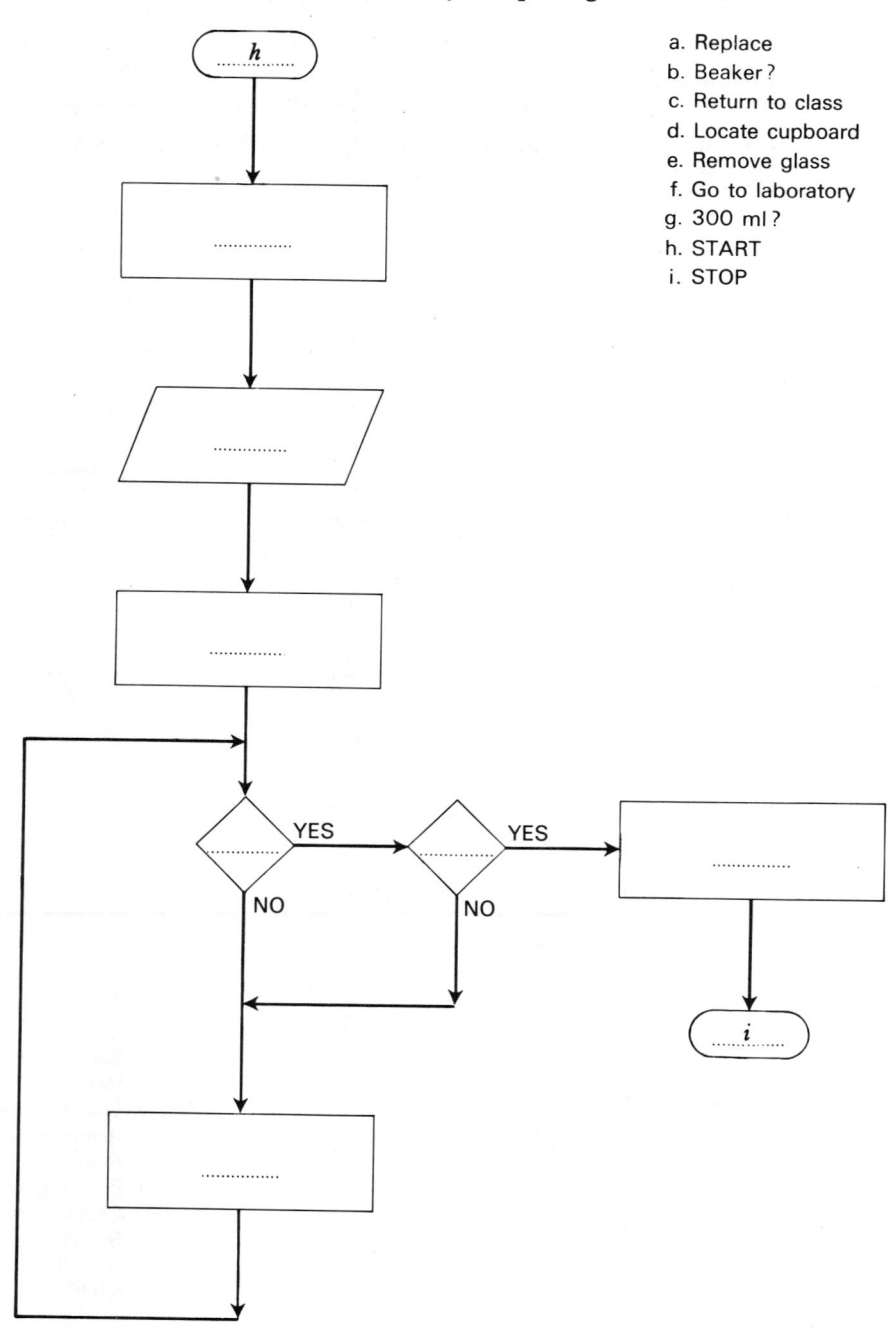

a. Replace
b. Beaker?
c. Return to class
d. Locate cupboard
e. Remove glass
f. Go to laboratory
g. 300 ml?
h. START
i. STOP

Problem 4.
Peter gets up in the morning, gets washed and dressed. Before having breakfast, he checks to see if the newspaper has been delivered. If it has, he takes it and puts it in the living room before sitting down to breakfast. After breakfast, he checks to make sure that he has completed all assigned homework. If there is still some to be done, he does it. Then he checks the clock, and if it is time to go, he leaves for the institute. If not, he reads the newspaper until it is time to go.

Flowchart Peter's activities by completing the flowchart below.

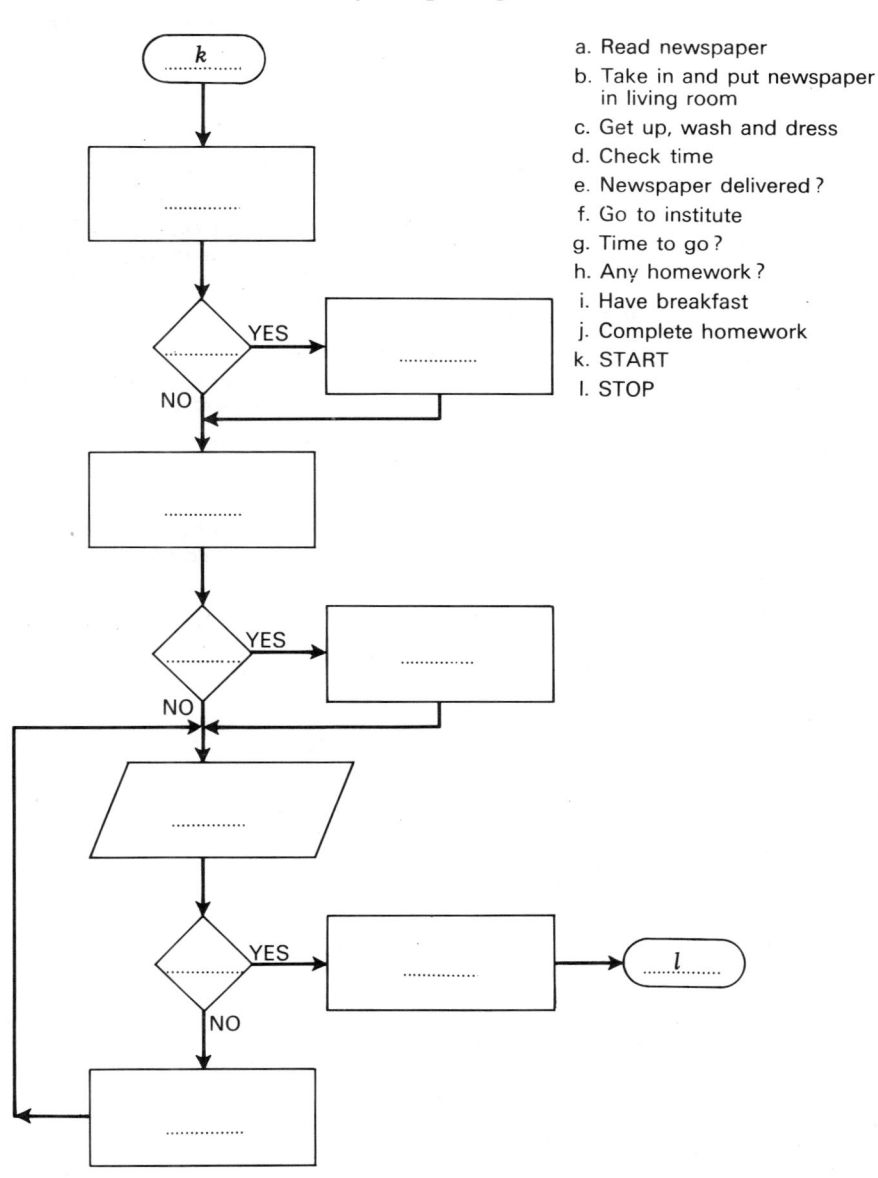

a. Read newspaper
b. Take in and put newspaper in living room
c. Get up, wash and dress
d. Check time
e. Newspaper delivered?
f. Go to institute
g. Time to go?
h. Any homework?
i. Have breakfast
j. Complete homework
k. START
l. STOP

8 Focus review

Focus M   Cause and effect

Read again 'Flowcharting' (Unit 20) to complete the table below.

PARA	CAUSE	EFFECT
[1]	if the finished program does not run as it should	
[2]		this is quite satisfactory
	if a permanent, neater and more readable flowchart is needed	
[3]		the word 'start' must be inserted inside the figure
	if it is the end of the program	
[4]		neither the flowchart nor the program can be done correctly
[5]	if documentation isn't available	
[6]		flowcharting is one of the first things a student programmer is taught

UNIT 21

Programs and programming languages

[1] Computers can deal with different kinds of problems if they are given the right instructions for what to do. Instructions are first written in one of the high-level languages, e.g. **FORTRAN, COBOL, ALGOL, PL/1, PASCAL** or **BASIC**, depending on the type of problem to be solved. A program written in one of these languages is often called a **source program**, and it cannot be directly processed by the computer until it has been **compiled**, which means interpreted into machine **code**. Usually a single instruction written in a **high-level** language, when transformed into machine code, results in several instructions. Here is a brief description of some of the many high-level languages:

FORTRAN acronym for FORmula TRANslation. This language is used for solving scientific and mathematical problems. It consists of algebraic formulae and English phrases. It was first introduced in the United States in 1954.

COBOL acronym for COmmon Business-Oriented Language. This language is used for commercial purposes. COBOL, which is written using English statements, deals with problems that do not involve a lot of mathematical calculations. It was first introduced in 1959.

ALGOL acronym for ALGOrithmic Language. Originally called IAL, which means International Algebraic Language. It is used for mathematical and scientific purposes. ALGOL was first introduced in Europe in 1960.

PL/1 Programming Language 1. Developed in 1964 to combine features of COBOL and ALGOL. Consequently, it is used for data processing as well as scientific applications.

BASIC acronym for Beginner's All-purpose Symbolic Instruction Code. Developed in 1965 at Dartmouth College in the United States for use by students who require a simple language to begin programming.

Other such languages are APL (developed in 1962) and PASCAL (named after Blaise Pascal and developed in 1971).

[2] When a program written in one of these high-level languages is designed to do a specific type of work such as calculate a company's payroll or calculate the stress factor on a roof, it is called an **applications** program. Institutions either purchase these programs as **packages** or commission their own programmers to write them to meet the specifications of the **users**.

[3] The program produced after the source program has been converted into machine code is referred to as an **object program** or object module. This is done by a computer program called the **compiler**, which is unique for each computer. Consequently, a computer needs its own compiler for the various high-level languages if it is expected to accept programs written in those languages. For example, in order that an IBM system 370 may process a program in FORTRAN, it needs to have a compiler that would understand that particular model and the FORTRAN language as well.

[4] The compiler is a **systems program**, which may be written in any language, but the computer's **operating system** is a true systems program which controls the central processing unit (CPU), the input, the output, and the secondary memory devices. Another systems program is the **linkage editor** which fetches required systems routines and links them to the object module (the source program in machine code). The resulting program is then called the **load module**, which is the program directly executable by the computer. Although systems programs are part of the software, they are usually provided by the manufacturer of the machine.

[5] Unlike systems programs, **software packages** are sold by various vendors and not necessarily by the computer manufacturer. They are a set of programs designed to perform certain applications which conform to internationally accepted rules, irrespective of the particular specifications of the user. Payroll is an example of such a package which allows the user to input data – hours worked, pay rates, special deductions, names of employees – and get salary calculations as output. These packages are coded in machine language (0s and 1s) on magnetic tapes or disks which can be purchased, leased or rented by users who choose the package that most closely corresponds to their needs.

Exercises

1 Main idea

Which statement best expresses the main idea of the text? Why did you eliminate the other choices?

- [ ] 1. Without software packages, it would be difficult to use the computer in solving problems such as payroll.
- [ ] 2. Compilers are indispensable to a computer.
- [ ] 3. Source programs written in high-level languages have to be changed to machine code before the computer can operate on them.

2 Understanding the passage

Decide whether the following statements are true or false (T/F) by referring to the information in the text. Then make the necessary changes so that the false statements become true.

T F
- [ ] [ ] 1. BASIC was developed to help students.
- [ ] [ ] 2. FORTRAN is very wordy and therefore not as efficient a computer language as COBOL in solving scientific problems.
- [ ] [ ] 3. All high-level programs must be translated to machine code before the computer can execute them.
- [ ] [ ] 4. The best place to buy software packages is from the manufacturer.
- [ ] [ ] 5. An example of an application program is calculating the stress on a roof.
- [ ] [ ] 6. An operating system program controls input and output operations.
- [ ] [ ] 7. Software packages are not written in high-level languages.
- [ ] [ ] 8. Different high-level languages suit different problems.
- [ ] [ ] 9. IBM machine code is the same as that of CDC.
- [ ] [ ] 10. It is a must for a programmer to be able to understand machine code.

3 Locating information

Find the passages in the text where the following ideas are expressed. Give the line references.

.... 1. Systems programs control the work of the computer system.
.... 2. Software packages are not always sold by the manufacturer.
.... 3. Usually, every high-level instruction translates into many more in machine code.
.... 4. Systems programs are usually provided by the manufacturer.
.... 5. Programmers may be required to write software for their employers.

4 Contextual reference

Look back at the text and find out what the words in **bold** typeface refer to.

1. If **they** are given the right   (l. 1) ....
2. **it** cannot be directly processed   (l. 6) ....
3. **it** is called an applications program   (l. 37) ....
4. commission **their** own programmers   (l. 39) ....
5. to write **them** to meet   (l. 39) ....
6. **that** would understand   (l. 48) ....
7. **which** controls the central   (l. 52) ....
8. links **them** to the object   (l. 55) ....
9. **They** are a set of programs   (l. 61) ....
10. **which** can be purchased   (l. 68) ....

5 Understanding words

Refer back to the text and find a synonym for the following words.

1. converted   (l. 9) ....
2. buy   (l. 38) ....
3. brings   (l. 54) ....
4. agree with, comply with   (l. 62) ....
5. rented   (l. 68) ....

Now refer back to the text and find an antonym for the following words.

6. lengthy   (l. 10) ....
7. unchanged   (l. 41) ....
8. separate   (l. 55) ....
9. reject   (l. 63) ....
10. depending on   (l. 63) ....

6 Word forms

First choose the appropriate form of the words to complete the sentences. Then check the differences of meaning in your dictionary.

1. instruction, instruct, instructed, instructor
   a. Our maths .... explained to us the principles of binary arithmetic.
   b. We were .... to document our programs very carefully.
   c. Both .... and data have to be changed to machine code before the computer can operate on them.

2. compilation, compiler, compile, compiled
   a. Our university computer does not have a PASCAL ....
   b. Usually, a programmer .... his program before he puts in the data.
   c. A source program cannot be directly processed by the computer until it has been ....

3. description, describe, described
   a. Our introductory programming text included a brief .... of the many high-level languages.
   b. It is difficult to .... the memory of a microcomputer without referring to 'chips'.

4. result, results, resulting
   a. The linkage editor links systems routines to the object module. The .... program, referred to as the load module, is directly executable by the computer.
   b. The .... of these mathematical operations were obtained from the university mainframe and not from my micro.

5. specification, specify, specific, specified, specifically
   a. Our company brought three packages with very .... applications: payroll, accounts receivable, and accounts payable.
   b. An applications program is designed to do a .... type of work, such as calculating the stress factor on a roof.
   c. Did the analyst give the new programmer the .... necessary to start on the project?

7a Content review

Match the following words in column A with the corresponding information in column B.

	A		B
☐	1. source program	a.	to solve a particular problem
☐	2. high-level languages	b.	can be executed by the computer directly
☐	3. applications program		
☐	4. software packages	c.	program translated to machine code
☐	5. object program	d.	connects routines with programs in memory
☐	6. compiler		
☐	7. systems program	e.	examples are COBOL and PASCAL
☐	8. operating systems		
☐	9. linkage editor	f.	directs the processes of the computer CPU, and peripherals
☐	10. load module		
		g.	groups of programs designed to solve a specific problem
		h.	written in a high-level language
		i.	computer needs one for each high-level language
		j.	deals with the running of the actual computer not with programming problems

7b Content review

Summarize the information on different high-level computer languages by completing the table below.

LANGUAGE	DEVELOPED	FUNCTION	CHARACTERISTIC
FORTRAN			
	1959		
		mathematical and scientific purpose	

Unit 21 *Programs and programming languages*

LANGUAGE	DEVELOPED	FUNCTION	CHARACTERISTIC
			combines features of COBOL and ALGOL
BASIC			
	1962		

8 Focus review

Read paragraphs 1 and 3 of 'Programs and Programming Languages' again – they are re-written below. What do the words in *italics* signify?

Computers can deal with different kinds of problems *if* they are given the right instructions for what to do. Instructions are first written in one of the high-level languages, *e.g.* FORTRAN, COBOL, ALGOL, PL/1, PASCAL, or BASIC, depending on the type of problem to be solved. A program written in one of these languages is often called a source program, and it cannot be directly processed by the computer *until* it has been compiled, which *means* interpreted into machine code. Usually a single instruction written in a high-level language, when transformed to machine code, *results in* several instructions. Here is a brief description of some of the many high-level languages: ...

a. *Cause-effect*
b. ....
c. ....
d. ....
e. ....

The program produced *after* the source program has been converted into machine code is *referred to as* an object program or object module. This is done by a computer program *called* the compiler, which is unique for each computer. *Consequently*, a computer needs its own compiler for the various high-level languages *if* it is expected to accept programs written in those languages. *For example, in order that* an IBM system 370 may process a program in FORTRAN, it needs to have a compiler that would understand that particular model and the FORTRAN language *as well*.

f. ....
g. ....
h. ....
i. ....
j. ....
k. ....
l. *Cause-effect*

m. ....

FOCUS N
Making predictions

A *prediction* is a statement about a particular subject which is related to a prior condition being fulfilled. It is a special kind of inference in which we tell in advance what we think will happen in the future. It is therefore impossible to predict without having any knowledge of an existing condition. By examining existing data, a logical conclusion can often be logically drawn about what is likely to happen next. Predictions of results based on existing conditions can be expressed as different levels of certainty. They are not absolute, and can change according to context. For example:

1. Certainty (100%) can be expressed by:

> will (definitely, certainly)
> certain, sure
> without a doubt, without question

2. Probability (75% – 90%) can be expressed by:

> probable, probably (75%)
> likely (75%)
> most probable, most probably, highly probable, most likely, highly likely (90%)

3. Possibility can be expressed by:

> may (not), might (not), can, could, possible, possibly, perhaps

4. Improbability (25%, 10%) can be expressed by:

> improbable, unlikely (25%)
> doubtful, questionable (25%)
> probably not (25%)
> most/highly improbable/
>   unlikely (10%)
> most/highly doubtful/
>   questionable (10%)
> most probably not 10%

5. Impossibility (0%) can be expressed by:

> a. present or future
>   cannot, could not
>   not possible, impossible
>
> b. past
>   could not
>   not possible, impossible

When a necessary condition exists in a process, the following expressions are used:

For Y to occur/happen/take place { X must be present or there must be Y
                                   Y depends on X

In a *condition-prediction relationship*, the statement of condition is preceded by **if** no matter to what degree of certainty the prediction is expressed.

Also the verb tenses are important to note because a distinction between the statement of condition which is made in the present must relate to the events of the prediction which will happen in the future.

Example

1. At the rate computer technology is growing, today's computers **might** be obsolete by 1985 and **most certainly** by 1990.

CONDITION	PREDICTION
At the rate computer technology is growing,	today's computers might be obsolete by 1985 and most certainly by 1990.

2. **If we couldn't feed information in and get results back, computers wouldn't be of much use.**

CONDITION	PREDICTION
If we couldn't feed information in and get results back,	computers wouldn't be of much use.

3. **If the hammer in drum printers hits a little early or late, the characters will appear slightly above or below the line.**

CONDITION	PREDICTION
If the hammer in drum printers hits a little early or late	the characters will appear slightly above or below the line.

Exercise 1

Read the following sentences and underline the part that expresses a condition, once; and the part expressing a prediction, twice.

1. It has been said that if transport technology had developed as rapidly as computer technology, a trip across the Atlantic Ocean today would take a few seconds.
2. Working for the U.S. Census Bureau, Dr. Hollerith realized that unless some means of speeding up the analyses of census data were found, it would take more than ten years to complete the job.
3. If the hammer in train printers hits a little early or late, the character will appear slightly to the right of its proper position.
4. Mainframes would still be occupying a lot of space if it weren't for microminiaturization.
5. If computer technology continues growing at the rate it has, bubble memory will soon replace the chip.

SECTION 8

Computer-related topics

UNIT 22

Time sharing versus batch

[1] The computer is a very expensive machine which is capable of executing jobs at an extremely fast rate. Since computer time is very costly, **time sharing** techniques were devised in order to use the central processing unit more efficiently by leaving it idle as little as possible. These techniques, of which **multiprogramming** is one, allow a number of users to share the resources of the computer concurrently. Multiprogramming is when more than one program can be present at different storage locations of the memory at the same time. When the CPU needs to work on a specific part of a program, it fetches it, processes it and, while the results are being printed or being stored on an on-line disk, the CPU fetches a part of another or the same program for processing. Consequently, although only one program is being executed at any one time, it is as though the CPU is working on various programs simultaneously. What actually happens is that the CPU is kept in action while programming operations, such as printing, are being carried out. The means by which the computer knows which programs to work on is determined by its operating system, which schedules and monitors the various programs being processed simultaneously.

[2] Computer systems capable of time sharing programs facilitate **real time** programming, which means that a user can interact with the computer by asking it to perform a desired task and have the task completed within a matter of seconds. An example of this is when an airline ticket reservation clerk, using a terminal, asks the computer about the availability of seats on a certain flight. In a few seconds the computer, having checked its updated **data bank**, gives back the answer.

[3] In real time processing, the user doesn't have to wait long to receive answers to his other questions. Moreover, an up-to-date view of the situation is provided. In contrast to real time processing, **batch** processing is done on programs which do not require interaction with the computer from a terminal, and which may involve lengthy input, output, and processing. Rather than being keyed in from a terminal, the input may come from cards, disk, or tape, while the output is usually on a high-speed printer. An example of a batch job is a computerized company payroll system.

Unit 22 Time sharing versus batch

Exercises

1 Main idea

Which statement best expresses the main idea of the text? Why did you eliminate the other choices?

☐ 1. Multiprogramming is a very efficient technique for using the central processing unit.

☐ 2. There are basically two ways of processing information by the computer: real time and batch mode.

☐ 3. Real time programming requires that information in data banks be constantly updated.

2 Understanding the passage

Decide whether the following statements are true or false (T/F) by referring to the information in the text. Then make the necessary changes so that the false statements become true.

T   F

☐ ☐ 1. The purpose of time sharing techniques is to make the best use of the CPU.

☐ ☐ 2. Real time processing allows interaction with the computer.

☐ ☐ 3. In multiprogramming, the programmer decides which programs the CPU should work on at any one moment.

☐ ☐ 4. In real time processing, data records should always be updated.

☐ ☐ 5. Data is inputted through a terminal for batch processing.

☐ ☐ 6. It is possible for the CPU to execute more than one program at any one time.

☐ ☐ 7. Real time processing takes a very short time compared to batch processing.

☐ ☐ 8. It is more practical for an airplane ticket reservation clerk to use batch rather than real time processing.

☐ ☐ 9. Batch processing is usually used if the output is expected to be long.

☐ ☐ 10. In multiprogramming, parts of the programs are kept in different storage places so that the CPU can work on them.

3 Locating information

Find the passages in the text where the following ideas are expressed. Give the line references.

.... 1. Interactive computing is very fast.
.... 2. The operating system tells the computer which program to work on.
.... 3. Input for batch processing is not usually done from the terminal.
.... 4. It is possible to have more than one user share the computer at the same time.
.... 5. For real time programming, information must be constantly updated.

4 Contextual reference

Look back at the text and find out what the words in **bold** typeface refer to.

1. **which** is capable of executing (l. 1) ....
2. by leaving **it** idle (l. 4) ....
3. **it** fetches it (l. 9) ....
4. processes **it** (l. 9) ....
5. **which** schedules and monitors (l. 17) ....
6. by asking **it** to perform (l. 21) ....
7. An example of **this** is when (l. 22) ....
8. having checked **its** updated (l. 25) ....
9. answers to **his** questions (l. 27) ....
10. and **which** may involve (l. 30) ....

5 Understanding words

Refer back to the text and find a synonym for the following words.

1. without work (l. 4) ....
2. simultaneously (l. 6) ....
3. particular (l. 9) ....
4. make easy (l. 19) ....
5. do (l. 21) ....

Now refer back to the text and find an antonym for the following words.

6. cheap (l. 2) ....
7. at different times (l. 8) ....
8. short (l. 30) ....

6 Word forms

First choose the appropriate form of the words to complete the sentences. Then check the differences of meaning in your dictionary.

1. execution, execute, executed, executive, executing
    a. A load module which is the result of system routines linked with an object module is directly .... by the computer.
    b. The time necessary for .... a program is usually indicated on the computer printout.
    c. An .... program consists of complex routines which are stored in the memory in order to supervise and control certain functions of the computer.

2. availability, available, availably
    a. Our university has a limited number of terminals installed. Consequently, it is not always easy to find one .... for use.
    b. The success of this course depends on the .... of the tutors to help the students in their computer assignments.

3. reservation, reserve, reserved
    a. Programming in COBOL requires the student to be familiar with a list of around 300 words called .... words.
    b. Computers are presently employed in on-line airline ticket ....

4. location, locate, located
    a. The memory of a computer has numerous storage .... called addresses.
    b. Have you been able to .... your error?

7 Content review

Try to think of a definition for each of these items before checking them in the Glossary. Then complete the following statements with the appropriate words. Make sure you use the correct form, i.e. singular or plural.

| data bank | multiprogramming | batch |
| time sharing | real time | |

1. If the .... of an airline is not updated, reservations would become very messy and complicated.
2. If more than one program or part of a program are present in the memory at the same time, this is called ....

3. .... processing is used when very long printouts are expected.
4. Multiprogramming is an example of ....
5. To be able to request information from the computer and get it quickly is called .... processing.

8 Focus review

1. Complete the table below by referring back to paragraph 1 of the text 'Time Sharing versus Batch'

Cause and effect/result		
MARKER	CAUSE	EFFECT/RESULT
since		
	these techniques	
		as though the CPU is working on various programs simultaneously

2. Complete the table below by referring back to paragraphs 1 and 3 of the text 'Time Sharing versus Batch'

Contrasting		
PARA	MARKER	ITEM CONTRASTED
1	although	
3		real time processing
3		

3. Complete the following table by referring back to paragraph 2 of 'Time Sharing versus Batch'.

TERM	EXPLANATION	EXAMPLE

Unit 22 Time sharing versus batch

4. Complete the table below by referring back to paragraph 3 of 'Time Sharing versus Batch'.

SITUATION	EVENT	MARKER	ADDITIONAL INFORMATION
	user doesn't have to wait for answers to questions		

5. Complete the table below by referring back to paragraph 3 of 'Time Sharing versus Batch'.

TERM	EXPLANATION	EXAMPLE
batch processing		

UNIT 23

Careers

[1] There is a wide range of jobs available in the field of data processing, the most common of which are **keypunch operator, computer operator, programmer, systems analyst,** and **data processing manager**.

[2] The keypunch operator must be both accurate and fast while punching programs and data onto cards. Moreover, he or she must be able to work under pressure when the workload in the data processing department is heavy. Recently, the introduction of terminals and screens has partly replaced the use of punched cards and, consequently, reduced the tasks performed by the keypunch operator.

[3] The computer operator should be a reliable person because the job involves responsibility for very expensive machines. His work is rather routine, like changing tapes and disks, but the operator should be mentally alert to cope with a multiprogramming environment which requires mixing many jobs, and be able to cope with emergency situations, if and when they arise. As soon as there is a malfunction in the system, the operator has to recognize it and report it to the manager, who would then advise the manufacturer. The operator's knowledge is mainly concerned with the hardware and not with the software, but he or she should have interest in programming and should know enough about it to be able to interpret the programmer's instructions. In very large and modern installations, the operator sits in front of a screen that shows an up-to-date summary of the computer jobs as they are being processed. The operator's duties have become so complex that certain programs called operating system (OS) which supervise the work of the computer are written to simplify the job. Often programmers start their careers as computer operators, and then slowly work their way up the ladder.

[4] The main tasks of a computer programmer are first, to write programs to solve problems; second, to write them on time as they are needed; and third, to write them clearly by fully documenting them so that other programmers can understand them. The kinds of problems that are tackled depend on whether the programmer is working for a computer manufacturer or user. The former needs such programs as compilers, **assemblers, executives,** operating systems, and **utility routines**. These programs are intermediaries between the machine and the commercial

programs which are written in one of the high-level languages. They are about the system, and therefore programmers who write them are called **systems programmers**. Manufacturers usually sell this kind of software along with their systems. If the programmer is working for a computer user, however, his or her programs may deal with either scientific or commercial problems.

[5] The career of a programmer can start as a **trainee** in a **data processing** department after a course in computer programming. At this stage, he or she is guided and supervised by another programmer. With increasing experience in writing more efficient programs, the trainee is given more responsibility and advances first to the position of a junior programmer and then to that of a senior programmer.

[6] **Specifications** for the data processing problems are given to the programmer by the systems analyst. The key to this person's job is communication, because he or she should be able to interact with the people in the department both verbally and in writing. Since one of the analyst's tasks is to analyse problems, outline solutions to them, and then delegate them to programmers to code, he or she must be able to express ideas regarding these problems clearly, thoroughly, and in writing. In addition, the analyst must have conversational ability since the job involves working with other people more often than working alone. The other aspect of this job deals with setting the objectives of a project and then finding the best method of achieving them. This involves constant examination of the system, modification of weaknesses in it, or sometimes even changing it to a completely new system.

[7] The key person in a data processing department is its manager. It is on his or her capacity as a leader as well as on his or her technical knowledge that the success of the department depends. The manager is responsible for communicating with his or her superiors regarding policy-making decisions of the organization, and regarding the services provided by the department. The manager should have the ability to comprehend technical writings related to the field in order to advise his or her superiors of the most recent developments in data processing which have a direct bearing on their problems. He or she should have enough practical data processing experience to ensure that everybody in the department, be it the analysts, the programmers, or the rest of the computer operations staff, are all working towards the same end. The manager should have an active mind, imagination, tact, and the ability to control others. The most important quality, though, is to remain calm and think clearly at times of crises.

Exercises

1 Main idea
Which statement best expresses the main idea of the text? Why did you eliminate the other choices?

- [ ] 1. There are various positions in a data processing department, all of which are very important.
- [ ] 2. The manager of a data processing department is the corner stone of the organization.
- [ ] 3. Programmers must be able to write programs, well and efficiently.

2 Understanding the passage
Decide whether the following statements are true or false (T/F) by referring to the information in the text. Then make the necessary changes so that the false statements become true.

T   F
- [ ] [ ] 1. The operator's job is not very creative, but it requires a lot of concentration.
- [ ] [ ] 2. Well-written programs must be documented in order that they may be used properly.
- [ ] [ ] 3. It is essential that the computer operator knows how to program.
- [ ] [ ] 4. A manager must remain composed when problems arise in order to make the right decisions.
- [ ] [ ] 5. Manufacturers usually sell the machines along with systems programs.
- [ ] [ ] 6. Although a manager does not need to program, he should be well informed about developments in the field of data processing.
- [ ] [ ] 7. Operating systems were designed to simplify the operator's job.
- [ ] [ ] 8. New projects are designated to programmers to analyse and work on.
- [ ] [ ] 9. When the computer breaks down, the operator reports the problem to the analyst.
- [ ] [ ] 10. The kind of program a programmer writes depends on who he is working for.

3 Locating information
Find the passages in the text where the following ideas are expressed.
Give the line references.

.... 1. A data processing manager must be informed about recent developments in the field.
.... 2. Operators need not know how to program.
.... 3. High-level languages are used to write commercial programs.
.... 4. An analyst determines the goals of a project.
.... 5. Because of the introduction of screens, cards are not used very frequently nowadays.

4 Contextual reference
Look back at the text and find out what the words in **bold** typeface refer to.

1. **His** work is   (l. 11) ....
2. **which** requires many   (l. 13) ....
3. if and when **they** arise (l. 15) ....
4. and report **it** to   (l. 16) ....
5. as **they** are being   (l. 22) ....
6. to write **them** on time (l. 29) ....
7. **The former** needs such (l. 33) ....
8. outline solutions to **them** (l. 52) ....
9. **which** have a direct   (l. 69) ....

5 Understanding words
Refer back to the text and find synonyms for the following words.

1. deal with   (l. 13) ....
2. a fault in operation (l. 15) ....
3. communicate   (l. 50) ....
4. orally   (l. 51) ....
5. alteration   (l. 59) ....

Now refer back to the text and find antonyms for the following words.

6. irresponsibility (l. 11) ....
7. cheap   (l. 11) ....
8. incapable   (l. 50) ....
9. failure   (l. 63) ....
10. lazy   (l. 73) ....

6 Word forms

First choose the appropriate form of the words to complete the sentences. Then check the differences of meaning in your dictionary.

1. mixture, mix, mixed, mixing, mixer
   a. I always get .... up between COBOL and BASIC. This results in syntax errors in my programs.
   b. The hexadecimal number system is a .... of numbers and letters.

2. supervision, supervise, supervised, supervisory, supervisor
   a. The .... is a program which is kept in the memory of a computer to control multiprogramming, timesharing, and input/output functions.
   b. The systems analyst insisted on .... the junior programmers for the first three months of their work.
   c. The project succeeded because of the careful .... by the data processing manager.

3. training, train, trained, training, trainer, trainee
   a. We have three new .... in our computer centre.
   b. It took him three years of .... to become an efficient programmer.
   c. .... in computer programming is offered by various educational institutions in the evening.
   d. It took me two weeks to .... myself to use the word processor. Now I can edit letters using my micro.

4. modification, modify, modified
   a. There are numerous problems in updating the existing payroll system due to .... that were made to the file structure.
   b. Lately, a lot of programs were .... to improve their efficiency.

7 Content review

Write the appropriate words for the following definitions.

1. a computer typist ....
2. responsible for reporting malfunctions in the system ....
3. translates outlined solutions to computer instructions ....
4. writes specifications that outline solutions to problems ....
5. must be a good leader and a rational thinker ....
6. writes programs that run the CPU and control its functions ....

Projections

Over the past thirty years, every day has brought with it new technological developments in the field of computers. Nowadays, memories have become smaller in size but are more powerful than their predecessors; for example, the memory of the 16-bit microcomputer which is already on the market has full minicomputer power and yet sells very cheaply. Another example is the CPU of the mainframe which used to do a few hundred cycles per second but now is capable of a billion such operations in the same time. Moreover, the cost is cheap enough to make mainframe data processing readily available to a larger section of society. Peripherals have not lagged behind in development either.

Where will all this lead? Most probably, computers will become so inexpensive that they will be applied to almost every aspect of modern living whether it is the classroom, the kitchen or the office. Already, it is difficult to envisage schools without computers to assist in the learning process. The computer is actually a multi-functional machine. For the student, it can be a laboratory workbook, a personal tutor, a visual demonstrator of scientific phenomena, a simulation model of real systems as well as a recreational facility full of fun and games. For the teacher, it can be a gradebook computing grades for entire classes and analysing the progress of individual students. For the school administrator, it is an invaluable tool in registering students, scheduling classes, generating monthly or yearly reports in addition to computing accounts and updating them at regular intervals. With the improved field of satellite communication, specialized distant education has already become more of a reality than a thing of the future. In California, the governor has called for a curriculum for every student to include the 'three C's' (computing, calculating, and communicating through technology) instead of the traditional 'three R's' (reading, writing, and 'rithmetic). In Japan, computer education is compulsory for high school graduation.

Countries that mass produce chips, such as Singapore, are already talking about an electronic society in which most of the heavy repetitive tasks are accomplished by electronic means or at least aided by them. Bank transfers, international scheduling of meetings, electronic correspondence, security surveillance, home control and so on are but some of the possible applications of computers as we know them and of microprocessor chips. The list seems to be inexhaustible.

But how will this affect our lives? The answer to this question is particularly difficult because it is not divorced from our attitudes towards this new technology. It is predicted that the effects will be similar to those generated by the introduction of television. Very soon, almost everyone will be in possession of one type of computer or another, whether it is the waiter in a restaurant who will rely on a calculator-like device to communicate the client's choice of menu to the chef, or the individual at home who will access a data base to get updated information on airline reservations, movies, theatres, doctor's appointments and the like.

Because of all these extensive applications of computers to the various spheres of life, the emphasis has shifted from the specialist to the user. In the very near future, the users will be able to define their problems at the CRT and through a system of networks. They will be able to interact with the machines to find immediate solutions to their problems. The key word to tomorrow's computerization will be decentralization and a shift towards more specialized distribution data processing networks.

GLOSSARY

A

Abacus An ancient instrument used for calculations. It consists of beads which are moved from left to right. (Unit 2)

Access (verb) To get information which is on a storage medium such as tape, disk or main memory. (Unit 11)

Access arm A device which positions the recording heads of a disk drive so that they can obtain data from a disk. (Unit 15)

Address The identification of the storage locations in primary memory. (Unit 11)

Algol A high-level programming language used for mathematical and scientific purposes. An acronym for ALGOrithmic Language. (Unit 21)

Algorithm A straightforward sequence of steps or instructions used to solve a problem. A program is an algorithm. (Unit 21)

Analog A computer that can simulate different measurements by electronic means. It continuously works out calculations. (Units 2, 6)

Applications program A program written in a high-level language. It is designed to do a specific type of work such as calculate a company's payroll. (Unit 21)

Applications software Programs designed to solve a specific problem, e.g. payroll. (Unit 5)

Arithmetic-Logical Unit (ALU) One of the components of the CPU. It is made up of electronic circuitry which performs the actual arithmetic and logical operations asked for by a program. (Units 9, 10)

Arithmetic unit The same as arithmetic-logical unit.

Assembler A systems program which is an intermediary between the machine and the commercial programs which are written in a high-level language. (Unit 21)

B

Backup system A system which provides a service when service is lost from another source. For example, cards are used as a backup system in case of loss of data from disks or tapes. (Unit 13)

Basic A high-level programming language which is used mainly for writing programs in conversational mode. An acronym for Beginner's All-purpose Symbolic Instructional Code. (Unit 21)

Batch A set of jobs which do not require interaction with the computer from a terminal and are all processed in one computer run. The input may come from cards, disks or tapes. (Unit 22)

Binary Pertaining to a pair; in computer terminology it refers to 0 and 1. (Unit 19)

Binary arithmetic Arithmetic which uses only two numbers, either 0 or 1. (Units 10, 19)

Binary digit A digit in the binary system which is either 0 or 1; usually referred to as bit. (Unit 19)

Binary system A number system which is based on two numbers 0 or 1. it is used by digital computers. (Unit 19)

Bits Binary digit which is either 0 or 1. Eight bits equal 1 byte. (Units 7, 11, 15, 19)

Block A physical group of data records on a tape or a disk. A number of blocks form a file. (Unit 14)

Block diagram A diagrammatic representation of the sequence of events to be followed in solving a problem. A synonym for a flowchart. (Unit 18)

BPI (Bytes Per Inch) A measure of the density of a tape. (Unit 14)

Breakdown Same as computer breakdown. (Unit 23)

Bugs The errors in a program. (Unit 18)

Bubble memory Consists of creating a thin film of metallic alloys over a board. When this film is magnetized, it produces magnetic bubbles, the presence or absence of which represents bits of information. (Unit 12)

Byte A group of 8 binary digits or bits which are considered as one unit. 1024 bytes equal 1K. (Unit 11)

C

CAI (Computer-Assisted Instruction) The use of the computer for individualized learning and correction whereby the student sits in front of a terminal and goes through a lesson at his own pace. (Unit 17)

CAL (Computer-Assisted Learning) Same as computer-assisted instruction. (Unit 17)

Card Same as punched card. (Units 1, 13)

Card reader An input device used to read the information represented by holes in a punched card in order to transmit it to the memory of the computer. (Units 1, 11)

Cartridge A circular disk called a platter which is about the same size as a long-playing phonograph record, which can be magnetized on both sides. (Units 7, 15)

Cassette A specialized audio cassette used to store data. (Unit 15)

Cathode Ray Tube Terminal (CRT) A visual display unit similar to a television screen using an electronic vacuum tube called the cathode ray tube to output data from the computer. (Units 1, 17)

Central Processing Unit (CPU) The brain of the computer which consists of three components: the memory, the arithmetic-logical unit and the control unit. It controls and carries out instructions given to the computer. (Units 5, 9)

Chain An impact printer which is also referred to as a train printer in which the characters move laterally across the pages and as the proper character moves into position, it is hammered onto the paper through a carbon ribbon. (Unit 16)

Channel Same as track. (Unit 15)

Chip A square or rectangular piece of silicon upon which several layers of an integrated circuit are etched. It is used in microcomputers. (Unit 2)

Circuit A combination of electrical devices and conductors that form a conducting path. (Unit 1)

Circuit board A board containing integrated circuits which make up the processor, memory and electronic controls for the peripheral equipment of microcomputers. (Unit 8)

Clock A component of the control unit; it produces very rapid electronic timing marks at regular intervals. (Unit 10)

Cobol A high-level programming language which is used for commercial applications. An acronym for Common Business-Oriented Language. (Unit 21)

Code The representation of information-data and instructions in symbolic language. (Unit 21)

Coding sheets Specially designed forms on which a program is written before transferring it to an input medium. (Unit 18)

Compile To interpret a source program or a list of instructions into machine language. (Unit 21)

Compiler A systems program which may be written in any language. It is used to convert a source program into machine code. Each high-level language has its own compiler. (Unit 21)

Computer breakdown Failure of the hardware which necessitates the attention of the service personnel. (Unit 23)

Computer installation It is a data processing center including the hardware, software, and the buildings and offices necessary for building input/output media. (Unit 6)

Computer operator A person who is physically responsible for operating the computer. He arranges tapes and disks. (Unit 23)

Computer science The science of studying the computer, how it functions and how to operate and program it. (Introduction)

Computer systems The central processing unit and the peripherals working together as a useful whole constitute the hardware components of a computer system. (Units 4, 5)

Glossary

Console A typewriter like a machine with a screen which allows the operator to communicate with the computer and get an up-to-date view of the jobs being processed. (Units 7, 9)

Contents The information or data which is kept at a particular storage location in memory. (Unit 11)

Control Unit (CU) One of two components of the CPU in digital computers. It transmits coordinating control signals and commands to the computer. (Unit 9)

Core A small ferrite ring which is capable of being magnetized and demagnetized in the memory of a computer. (Units 1, 11, 12)

Core memory A computer memory which is made up of cores. (Unit 12)

Counter A component of the control unit; it selects instructions, one at a time, from memory. (Unit 10)

CRT display Same as cathode ray tube terminal. (Units 1, 17)

Cylinder A stack of tracks on a group of platters in a disk. (Unit 15)

D

Daisy wheel printer An impact printer which uses a wheel with up to 100 characters each being on an individual arm, so that only rotation is needed for the hammer to hit each letter. It has superb print quality. (Unit 16)

Data The information that is inputted with the program, and on which mathematical and logical operations are performed. (Unit 1)

Data bank All the organized data available to a particular institution. (Unit 22)

Data base A file of data which is structured in such a way to satisfy the needs of various users and not only one specific application.

Data base management To structure and organize data such that the requirements of various users are met without the need to duplicate the data.

Data pack Disks with the recording heads sealed inside instead of being attached to the disk drive. (Unit 15)

Data processing Handling or manipulating information called data which is specially prepared to be understood by the computer. This involves clerical functions as well as arithmetic and logical operations performed by the computer. (Unit 6)

Data processing manager The person who directs a data processing department. He should have leadership qualities as well as some technical knowledge of the field. (Unit 23)

Decimal system A number system which is based on 10 digits: 0, 1, 2, 3, 4, 5, 6, 7, 8 and 9. (Unit 19)

Decision-making To formulate judgments and conclusions regarding any issue. (Unit 4)

Deck A stack of cards which constitute one group, e.g. the punched cards that make up one program. (Unit 13)

Decoder A component of the control unit; it takes the coded instruction and breaks it down into the individual commands necessary to carry it out. (Unit 10)

Dedicated function A function which is performed numerous times by a mini or a micro. (Unit 11)

Density The number of bytes that can be stored on one inch of tape. It is measured by bytes per inch (BPI). (Unit 4)

Device Something invented or adapted for a specific purpose. (Unit 1)

Diamond symbol ◇ One of the symbols on a template used in flowcharting to indicate that a decision has to be made. (Unit 20)

Digit A number which has only one character, 0, 1, 2, 3, 4, 5, 6, 7, 8, or 9. (Unit 6)

Digital computer A computer in which information is represented by one of two electronic states: on or off. These are represented by the two digits 1 and 0 respectively. (Units 2, 6)

Disk A storage device which is made up of one or more circular plates which can be magnetized on both sides. Disks can be either floppy or hard. (Units 1, 15)

Disk drive A device which is capable of transmitting magnetic impulses representing data from the disk to the computer memory and vice versa. (Units 1, 15)

Diskette Same as floppy disk. (Unit 15)

Display screen A visual display unit like a T.V. screen used for the visual output of the data. (Unit 17)

Drum An impact printer which has a spinning cylinder for each character position in a line, and each cylinder containing all the characters in a character set. (Unit 16)

Dual-density A screen which has the possibility of showing two different light densities: light and dark. (Unit 17)

Dynamic graphics Graphics that show movement. (Unit 17)

E

Electrosensitive printers Same as thermal printers. (Unit 16)

Electrostatic plotter A device which electronically generates patterns of dots in a line across a page to make up a picture. (Unit 17)

Execute To run the instructions of a program after they are changed to the machine code by the compiler. (Unit 20)

Executive A systems program which consists of a number of routines that are kept either partly or totally in the main memory so as to control and supervise certain functions of the computer.

F

Fibre optics The field of telecommunications which uses instead of copper wires, plastic ribbons containing hair-thin optical fibres made from transparent glass. Sound is transmitted as light pulses instead of electrical signals.

File A group of blocks which, in turn, is a group of records. (Unit 14)

Fixed-head disk Hard magnetic disks are two types: fixed-head and moving-head. (Unit 15)

Fixed application A program written to solve one specific problem. (Unit 7)

Floppy disk Also called diskettes which are made from plastic. They are very light, flexible and inexpensive and are usually used with microcomputers. (Unit 15)

Flowchart A diagram or a sequence of steps which represent a solution of a problem. Arrows are used to show the sequence of events. (Unit 18)

Fortran A high-level programming language which is used for mathematical and scientific problems. An acronym for FORmula TRANslation. (Unit 21)

Frame A vertical pattern on the magnetic tape. It consists of eight bits of data plus one bit for error detection. (Unit 14)

G

General-purpose computer A computer which can be programmed to solve various types of problems. It is also called all-purpose computer. (Unit 4)

Graphics Line drawings which are used to illustrate a point or tell a story. (Unit 17)

H

Hard-copy terminal A terminal which outputs information on paper. (Unit 17).

Hard disk Disks which are made from a hard material and are of two kinds: moving-head and fixed-head. (Unit 15)

Hardware The physical, electronic and electromechanical devices which constitute the computer. (Unit 3, 5)

Hexadecimal system A number system which is based on 16 digits, 0, 1, 2, 3, 4, 5, 6, 7, 8, 9, A, B, C, D, E, F. (Unit 19)

High-level language A language in which each instruction represents several machine code instructions. It uses notation which is readable by a programmer. Examples are Cobol and Basic. (Unit 21)

Hub The hole or socket in control panel through which electrical impulses may be emitted or into which impulses may be sent. (Unit 15)

Hybrid computer A scientific computer system which incorporates characteristics of the digital and analog computers. (Unit 6)

I

Impact printer A printer which is based on the method of striking characters through a carbon like a typewriter. Examples are the drum, chain, daisy wheel, matrix and line printers. (Unit 16)

Ink jet printer A non-impact printer which operates by projecting small ink droplets and deflecting them electrostatically. (Unit 16)

Input The information which is presented to the computer. (Unit 3)

Input device Machines by which information is sent to the computer, e.g. a card reader. (Unit 5)

Instruction A part of a computer program which tells the computer what to do at that stage. (Unit 1)

Interactive Also conversational; to be able to communicate with the computer on a question and answer basis. (Unit 7)

Inter Block Gap (IBG) Special characters used on a tape to separate one block of information from another. (Unit 14)

Internal memory Same as primary memory. (Units 9, 11)

Internal storage Same as internal memory, main storage or primary memory. (Unit 11)

Inter Record Gap (IRG) Special characters used on a tape to separate one record of information from another. (Unit 14)

Interrupt feature When a program is interrupted upon receiving a signal indicating that any one of a number of external events has occurred. (Unit 7)

J

Job Control Language (JCL) A language associated with an operating system. It is used to write the instructions to control a job in a specific system. (Unit 21)

K

K 1024 bytes. (Unit 11)

Keyboard A device like a typewriter with keys representing different characters. The depression of the keys cause a hole to be punched in a card or a signal to be transmitted to the computer. (Unit 3)

Keypunch A machine with a keyboard used for punching data on cards. (Unit 13)

Keypunch operator A person who operates a keypunch in order to transfer the instructions in a program onto cards. (Units 13, 23)

L

Laser writer A non-impact printer in which the paper is charged electrostatically and attracts dry ink powder as in a Xerox machine. The pattern is then baked on the paper. (Unit 16)

Limitations The things a person or a machine cannot do. (Unit 4)

Line printer An impact printer having the character set to be printed on a cylinder, each segment of which has the full set of characters in raised form around the edges. (Unit 16)

Linkage editor A systems program which fetches required systems routines and links them to the object module (the source program in machine code). (Unit 21)

Load module The program which is directly executable by the computer. (Unit 21)

Logarithmic tables Tables which show the exponent of the power to which a fixed number must be raised to produce a given number. (Unit 2)

Logical unit Same as arithmetic-logical unit; it is responsible for carrying out logical operations on data. (Units 9, 10)

Low-level languages A language such as the assembly language in which each instruction has one corresponding instruction in machine code. (Unit 21)

M

Machine code Machine language. (Unit 21)

Magnetic tape A strip of plastic usually half an inch wide, coated on one side with metal oxide that can be magnetized. It stores information sequentially. (Units 1, 11 14)

Magnetic tape cartridge A memory storage device used with minicomputers. (Unit 7)

Mainframe A large computer system which is found in large installations processing immense amounts of data. (Unit 6)

Main storage Same as primary memory.

Matrix printer An impact printer which uses pins to print a pattern of dots on paper. The characters are generated by selecting the appropriate combination of pins. (Unit 16)

Medium The means by which something is done. Examples of input media are punched cards, magnetic tapes and disks. (Unit 1)

Memory The internal storage locations of a computer. It is also called real storage or primary memory. (Units 1, 11)

Memory board Same as circuit board. (Unit 8)

Memory unit Refers to the backing store media such as magnetic tape or magnetic disk.

Micro Same as microcomputer. (Unit 8)

Microcomputer A microcomputer which is based upon an integrated circuit microprocessor; also called computer-on-a-chip. (Unit 8)

Microminiaturization To make things on a very small scale. (Unit 2)

Microprocessor The central processing unit of a microcomputer. It is built as a single semiconductor device. (Units 7 & 8)

Mini Same as minicomputer. (Unit 7)

Minicomputer A computer whose mainframe is physically small, has a fixed word length between 8 and 32 bits and costs less than $100,000 for the central processor. (Unit 7)

Miniperipheral Peripherals specially developed for minicomputers, e.g. magnetic tape cartridges and cassettes. (Unit 7)

Monochromatic Shades of one colour only. (Unit 17)

Moving-head disk Hard disks which can be divided into either cartridge or pack. (Unit 15)

Multiplexing In the field of fibre optics, to combine a number of signals and carry them on one optical link.

Multiprogramming A time sharing technique which allows more than one user to share the resources of the computer. It is when more than one program can be present at different storage locations of the memory at the same time. (Unit 22)

N

Non-impact printer A printer which is based on the method of photocopying like an office copier. Examples are thermal, electrosensitive, ink jet printers and laser writers. (Unit 16)

O

Object program The program produced after the source program has been converted into machine code. Also called object module. (Unit 21)

Octal system A number system which is based on 8 digits, 0, 1, 2, 3, 4, 5, 6, 7. (Unit 19)

Off When no electric current passes through. (Unit 19)

Off-line When any part of a computer system operates independently of the central processing unit, it is said to be off-line. (Unit 13)

On When an electric current passes through. (Unit 19)

On-line When any part of a computer system is hooked up to and controlled by the central processing unit, it is said to be on-line. (Unit 13)

Operating systems A systems program which controls the central processing unit, the input, the output and the secondary memory devices. (Unit 21)

Operator The person who is responsible for the manual control operations of the computer. He is mainly concerned with hardware. (Unit 9)

Glossary

Output The results of performing arithmetic and logical operations on data. It is transmitted by the computer to a physical medium such as cards, tapes or disks. (Unit 3)

Output devices Machines by which information is received from the computer, e.g. a disk drive. (Unit 5)

P

Pack A hard disk which is made up of a number of platters. (Unit 15)

Package A generalized program which is written for a particular application such as an inventory package. (Unit 21)

Parallelogram ▱ It is one of the symbols on a template used in flowcharting to indicate the input or output. (Unit 20)

Parity bit The ninth bit of a frame on a magnetic tape. It is used for error detection. (Unit 14)

Pascal A high-level programming language which was developed in 1971 and named after Blaise Pascal. (Unit 21)

Peripherals Devices which are used with the computer. They can be on-line or off-line, and are used for input and output purposes. (Units 3, 5)

Platter A circular disk which is the same size as a long-playing phonograph record, and which can be magnetized on both sides. (Unit 15)

PL/1 A high-level programming language used for both scientific and commercial applications. An acronym for Programming Language 1. (Unit 21)

Plotter A pen-like device which draws graphs on paper for visual display of information. (Unit 17)

Primary memory The internal storage locations of a computer; also referred to as main memory or real storage. (Units 8, 11)

Primary storage Same as main storage. (Unit 7)

Printer An output device which changes the output data into printed form. (Units 3, 16)

Printout The printed pages which are the output from a printer. (Unit 18)

Priority A system used in multiprogramming to determine the sequence in which programs are to be processed.

Processing It is manipulating the information which is inputted to the computer by performing arithmetic or logical operations on it. (Unit 3)

Processor The same as central processing unit. (Units 3, 5)

Program A list of instructions which are used by the computer to solve a problem. (Unit 1)

Program documentation Detailed instructions for the use and interpretation of a program. (Unit 20)

Programmer The person who prepares the instructions for the computer. (Unit 4)

Programming Writing programs for the computer. (Unit 6)

Punched card A rectangular card with 12 rows and 80 columns which can be punched. It is used to input information into the computer or to receive the outputted result. (Units 1, 13)

R

Random access When any part of the memory may be read or accessed equally quickly. (Unit 11)

Random access device A device such as a magnetic disk drive which allows random accessing of information. (Unit 11)

Real storage Same as internal storage or primary memory. (Unit 11)

Real time When a user can interact with the computer by asking it to perform a desired task and have the task completed within a matter of seconds. (Unit 22)

Real time application Applications which require real time processing such as airline reservations. (Unit 7)

Real time processing Processing of data as soon as they are generated and using these data to update the relevant files. The opposite is batch processing. (Unit 7)

Record A group of frames which represent a unit of information such as a transaction. (Unit 14)

Recording heads The read and write heads of drives which access information from tapes or disks. (Unit 15)

Rectangle ☐ It is one of the symbols in a template used in flowcharting to stand for a processing action. (Unit 20)

Reel A spool in the tape drive upon which a magnetic tape is mounted. (Unit 14)

Register A component of the control unit; it temporarily holds the instruction read from memory while it is being executed. (Unit 10)

Robot A manlike machine which is manufactured to do the manual, routine and mechanical work for people. (Unit 18)

S

Screen The part of a visual display unit on which the program, data, and graphics can be seen. (Unit 1)

Schema The complete description of the logical structure of the data. (Unit 23)

Secondary memory Storage space which is outside the main memory of the computer. It can be either sequential (tapes) or random-access (disks). (Units 3, 1)

Semiconductor A material which is neither a good nor a bad conductor of electricity. Its conductivity increases at high temperatures. Transistors are made up of semiconductor material. (Units 8, 12)

Semiconductor memory Also referred to as chip, consists of thousands of integrated circuits etched onto a tiny piece of silicon with semi-conductor characteristics. It is used mostly in microcomputers. (Unit 12)

Sequential device A device such as the magnetic tape drive which permits information to be written onto or read off some storage medium in a fixed sequence only. (Unit 11)

Sets of data Organized groups of data. (Unit 22)

Shared-logic A computer system where the CPU controls the printers and screens which are not very intelligent on their own.

Shared resource When various stand-alones are linked to one resource such as a big disk drive. They are capable of resuming operations even if the main source fails.

Single purpose Used for only one purpose. (Unit 3)

Slide rule An instrument used for calculations. Numbers are represented by lengths on a ruler and arithmetic operations are performed on them by sliding another part of the ruler. (Unit 2)

Software The programs that control and coordinate the activities of the computer hardware and that direct the processing of the data. (Unit 5)

Software packages A set of programs designed to perform certain applications which conform to internationally accepted rules. An example is payroll packages. (Unit 21)

Source program A program written in one of the high-level languages such as Fortran and Cobol. (Unit 21)

Specifications Detailed description of solutions to problems which are given by the analyst to the programmer to be translated into a program. (Unit 23)

Spooling Information is first punched on cards, then transferred to tape or disk before it is transmitted to the computer. (Unit 3)

Stand-alone A self-contained computer unit with its CPU and storage.

Storage device A device on which information can be stored. (Unit 3)

Sub-schema The description of the parts of a schema (the logical structure of the data). (Unit 23)

Systems analyst The person who analyses problems, outlines solutions to them, and then delegates them to programmers to code. (Unit 23)

Systems program A program written for the computer system. Examples are compilers, operating systems, and linkage editors. They are usually provided by the manufacturer. (Unit 21)

Systems programmer A programmer who writes programs that control the computer system such as assemblers, executives and utility programs. (Unit 23)

Systems software The programs which direct the computer to perform tasks and control its operations. (Unit 5)

T

Tape See magnetic tape. (Units 1, 11, 14)

Tape drive A device on which a magnetic tape is mounted in order that information may be transmitted from the tape to the memory of the computer or vice versa. (Units, 1, 14)

Tape mark A special character which is used to separate one file of data from another. (Unit 14)

Template A sheet of plastic with all the flowcharting symbols cut into it. (Unit 20)

Terminal A device at which data is inputted to the computer or results outputted onto a screen or paper. (Units, 1, 17)

Terminal symbol ⊂⊃ The first and last symbol of a flowchart. It indicates the beginning or the end of a program. (Unit 20)

Thermal printer A non-impact printer which uses a special chemically treated paper on which the characters are exposed by such means as a laser. (Unit 16)

Time sharing To allow a number of users to share the sources of the computer concurrently. (Unit 22)

Track The channels of a magnetic tape on which information is recorded by tape drives. (Unit 14) Also the concentric circle of a disk, which are similar to the grooves in a record, and on which information is stored. (Unit 15)

Train Same as chain. (Unit 16)

Trainee A person with little or no work experience in the computer field who joins a data processing department and is supervised and guided by an experienced programmer. (Unit 23)

Transactions An event which requires the creation of a record, the updating of a file or its processing.

Transfer speed The number of bytes per second a tape drive is capable of transferring from the tape to the memory of a computer and vice versa. (Unit 14)

Transfer rate Same as transfer speed. (Unit 14)

Transistor A small semiconductor which operates as an amplifier. (Unit 2)

Turnkey systems They are systems software and applications software products. (Unit 5)

U

User An individual or a group making use of the output of the computer. (Unit 21)

Utility routine A systems program which performs operations on files: it recognizes files, transfers them from one medium of storage to another, etc. It is not concerned with the specific contents of the files. (Unit 23)

V

Vacuum tubes A closed glass electron tube with no air in it, used for controlling a flow of electricity as in radio or T.V. (Unit 2)

Virtual storage When disks are hooked up to the computer and used as an extension of internal storage in order to increase the capacity of primary memory. (Unit 11)

Visual display unit Same as cathode ray tube terminal. (Unit 1)

W

Word processing The use of a computerized typewriter to automate some of the secretarial tasks such as formatting and typing letters.

Z

Zone punch The top three rows on a card are called the zone punch rows. (Unit 13)

For further reference

The following books are recommended for both students and teachers to accompany the main coursebooks:

Oxford Advanced Learner's Dictionary of Current English
Revised and Updated   A. S. Hornby and A. P. Cowie

The *Oxford Advanced Learner's Dictionary of Current English* is recognized throughout the world as the indispensable reference book for those studying or teaching English as a second or foreign language. It gives special help in many areas of interest to foreign students not catered for in most dictionaries.

The definitions have all been written within a carefully controlled defining vocabulary and are reinforced and illustrated by over 90,000 contemporary example sentences and phrases which learners can use as models for their own work. This practical contribution to written and oral work makes the dictionary an ideal complement to any coursebook and provides the learner with an invaluable aid to self-study. The clear layout and careful design make all the information easy to find, easy to understand, and easy to use.

It contains:
* 50,000 headwords
* 11,000 idiomatic expressions
* 90,000 illustrative phrases and sentences
* 1,000 illustrations
* 10 appendices

Practical English Usage   Michael Swan

Practical English Usage is packed with information of enormous value and interest to all EFL students and teachers. It contains articles on all the grammatical problems which regularly cause difficulty to foreign learners, and explains points often not dealt with in other reference books. In addition, it covers selected problems of vocabulary, idiom, style, pronunciation, and spelling, with information about differences between British and American English where appropriate.

A Practical English Grammar   A. J. Thomson and A. V. Martinet

This is the most popular intermediate-level reference grammar for students and teachers of English. All the important areas of English are covered and the use of forms is illustrated by many thousands of modern example sentences. Points which students find particularly difficult, like tense forms and auxiliary verbs, are treated with especial care and fullness.

Also available: A Practical English Grammar Exercises 1 & 2
A Practical English Grammar Structure Drills 1 & 2

Other English for Specific Purposes Titles from Oxford University Press

Basic Technical English   J. Comfort, S. Hick, A. Savage

A reading course for beginner/elementary level students in secondary schools, vocational schools and colleges, or in-company training programmes. The main aim of the course is to develop confidence and ability in extracting information from technical manuals and textbooks in a wide range of technical areas.

A clear and detailed Teacher's Book accompanies the course.

Career   J. A. Blundell, N. M. G. Middlemiss

Career is a two-part beginner's course for English language learners working in the business, commercial, and professional world. *Career* deals with the basic structures and vocabulary of English and takes the learner to an intermediate level in all four skills: listening, reading, speaking, and writing. The course is set in the offices of a growing international company. Cassettes of the dialogues and drills are available and a comprehensive Teacher's Book accompanies each part of the course.

Manage with English   P. L. Sandler and C. L. Stott

Manage with English is an intermediate level course for managers and management trainees who need to use English professionally in the modern business world. The units cover a wide range of management topics based on personnel, production, marketing and finance, eg, Recruitment, Training, Research & Development, Company Organization, Advertising, Promotion, and Sales.
Manage with English carefully controls the presentation of structures and vocabulary in a business context, placing dual emphasis on how the language structure works and carries meaning, and on putting the language to practical use.

English for Travel   John Eastwood

English for Travel is intended for people whose level of English is at present very basic but who find that they need English in order to 'survive' on their travels. Whether on business or pleasure, there are certain key questions which the traveller abroad finds that he has to ask and English is often the only common language. He also has to cope with the often 'uncontrolled' language of the replies he receives. *English for Travel*

(Continues)

provides both the language and vocabulary needed to do these things by taking the learner through authentic travel situations such as he will encounter in real life.

English in Focus

Series editors: J. P. B. Allen and H. G. Widdowson

An important series for intermediate and advanced students of science, technology, and the humanities. *English in Focus* is designed for students who need to extend their knowledge of the language in order to cope with the kind of written English they will require for their specialist studies.

The following are a selection taken from the *English in Focus* series: English in Electronics and Electrical Engineering, English in Mechanical Engineering, English in Workshop Practice, English in Physical Science, and English in Education.

If you would like more information about any of these titles please write to:

English Language Teaching
Marketing Department
Oxford University Press
Walton Street
Oxford
OX2 6DP